GALATIANS & EPHESIANS

Also by Tara-Leigh Cobble

The Bible Recap:
A One-Year Guide to Reading and Understanding the Entire Bible

The Bible Recap Study Guide:
Daily Questions to Deepen Your Understanding of the Entire Bible

The Bible Recap Journal:
Your Daily Companion to the Entire Bible

The Bible Recap Discussion Guide:
Weekly Questions for Group Conversation on the Entire Bible

The Bible Recap Kids' Devotional:
365 Reflections and Activities for Children and Families

The God Shot:
100 Snapshots of God's Character in Scripture

Israel: *Beauty, Light, and Luxury*

The Bible Recap for Kids:
A 365-Day Guide Through the Bible for Young Readers

The Bible Recap 365-Day Chronological Study Bible:
English Standard Version

The Bible Recap Knowing Jesus Series*

Knowing Jesus as King: A 10-Session Study on the Gospel of Matthew

Knowing Jesus as Servant: A 10-Session Study on the Gospel of Mark

Knowing Jesus as Savior: A 10-Session Study on the Gospel of Luke

Knowing Jesus as God: A 10-Session Study on the Gospel of John

The Bible Recap Knowing God Series*

Acts: The Spirit and the Bride—
a 10-Week Bible Study on God and His Church

Romans: Dead to Sin and Alive to Christ—
a 10-Week Bible Study

1 & 2 Corinthians: Love, Unity, and the Countercultural
Power of the Cross—a 10-Week Bible Study

* General editor

THE BIBLE RECAP KNOWING GOD SERIES

GALATIANS & EPHESIANS

THE FREEDOM AND PURPOSE IN THE BODY OF CHRIST

A 10-WEEK BIBLE STUDY

TARA-LEIGH COBBLE,
GENERAL EDITOR

WRITTEN BY THE D-GROUP THEOLOGY & CURRICULUM TEAM

a division of Baker Publishing Group
Minneapolis, Minnesota

Published by Bethany House Publishers
Minneapolis, Minnesota
BethanyHouse.com

Bethany House Publishers is a division of
Baker Publishing Group, Grand Rapids, Michigan

Printed in the United States of America

ISBN 9780764243639 (paper)
ISBN 9781493446940 (ebook)

Library of Congress Cataloging-in-Publication Control Number: 2025016776

The D-Group Theology & Curriculum Team is Laura Buchelt, Emily Pickell, Abbey Dane, Kirsten McCloskey, Emma Dotter, Liz Suggs, and Tara-Leigh Cobble.

The general editor is represented by Alive Literary Agency, AliveLiterary.com.

Cover design by Dan Pitts

Baker Publishing Group publications use paper produced from sustainable forestry practices and postconsumer waste whenever possible.

25 26 27 28 29 30 31 7 6 5 4 3 2 1

CONTENTS

HOW TO USE THIS STUDY

While Bible study is vital to the Christian walk, a well-rounded spiritual life comes from engaging with other spiritual disciplines as well. This study is designed not only to equip you with greater knowledge and theological depth, but to help you engage in other formative practices that will create a fuller, more fulfilling relationship with Jesus. We want to see you thrive in every area of your life with God!

Content and Questions

In each of the ten weeks of this study, the teaching and questions are divided into six days, but feel free to do it all at once if that's more manageable for your schedule. If you choose to complete each week's study in one sitting (especially if that time occurs later in the study-week), keep in mind that there are aspects you will want to be mindful of each day: the daily Bible reading, Scripture memorization, and the weekly challenge. Those are best attended to throughout the week.

Daily Bible Reading

The daily Bible reading corresponds to our study. It will take an average of three minutes per day to simply read (not study) the text. If you're an auditory learner, you may prefer to listen to an audio version of these Bible chapters.

Even if you decide to do the week's content and questions in one sitting, we still encourage you to make the daily Bible reading a part of your regular daily rhythm. Establishing a habit of reading the Word every day will help fortify your faith and create greater connection with God.

If you decide to break the study up into the six allotted days each week, your daily Bible reading will align with your study. Days 1–5 will follow our study of Galatians and Ephesians, Day 6 features a psalm that corresponds to our reading, and Day 7 serves as a catch-up day in case you fall behind.

Scripture Memorization

Memorizing Scripture isn't busywork! It's an important part of hiding God's Word in our hearts (Psalm 119:11). Our first memorization passage—Galatians 5:13–17—focuses on using our freedom in Christ to serve others rather than ourselves. And our second memorization passage—Ephesians 6:13–18a—centers on the necessity of the armor of God in the life of faith. We encourage you to practice the verses cumulatively—that is, *add* to what you're practicing each week instead of *replacing* it. We quote the English Standard Version (and some of our resources are in that translation as well), but feel free to memorize them in whatever translation you prefer. We suggest working on each week's verse(s) throughout the week, not just at the last minute. We've provided some free tools to help you with this, including a weekly verse song: MyDGroup.org/Resources/GalEph.

Weekly Challenge

This is our practical response to what we've learned each week. We want to be "doers of the word, and not hearers only" (James 1:22). You'll find a variety of challenges, and we encourage you to lean into them all—especially the ones you find *most* challenging! This will help strengthen your spiritual muscles and encourage you in your faith. As with the memory verse, you'll want to begin this practice earlier in the week, especially because some weekly challenges include things to do each day of the week (e.g., prayers, journaling, etc.).

Resources

This is a Scripture-heavy study, and you'll find yourself looking up passages often. If you're new to studying Scripture, this will be a great way to dig in and sharpen your skills! You will feel more equipped and less intimidated as you move through each chapter. Some questions may ask you to refer to a Bible dictionary, commentary, or Greek or Hebrew lexicon, but you don't need to purchase those tools. There are lots of free options available online. We've linked to some of our favorite tools—plus additional resources such as podcasts, articles, and apps—at MyDGroup.org/Resources/GalEph.

Groups

Because each week has a lot of questions in the content, we offer the following recommendation for those who plan to discuss the study in a weekly group meeting. As each member is doing their homework, we suggest they mark their favorite items with a star and mark any confusing items with a question mark. This serves as preparation for the group discussion and helps direct the conversation in beneficial ways. Group leaders, please note the starred prompts in each chapter; we've highlighted these for you as topics you may find helpful to prioritize in group discussions.

INTRODUCTION TO GALATIANS

Paul visited the cities collectively known as Galatia on each of his missionary journeys. In these cities there was a group of well-known churches that Paul loved deeply. Out of his great love for them, he pulled no punches when it came to criticizing and admonishing their mishandling of the gospel.

There are two primary theories on where this area of Galatia was. It may have been in south central Turkey, in which case this letter was likely written from Corinth during Paul's second missionary journey (approximately AD 52). Or Galatia may have been in north central Turkey, in which case Paul probably penned this letter from Ephesus during his third missionary journey (approximately AD 57). Fortunately, identifying the original audience has little bearing on the interpretation of the letter today.

This letter is devoid of some of Paul's typical introductory greetings and warm wishes; his tone is firm but loving. He offered strong criticism to those who tried to require circumcision for Gentile believers. But don't miss his point—this message wasn't ultimately about circumcision; that was merely the surface issue that pointed to a deeper problem. His primary concern was that false teachers were attempting to add requirements for salvation, thus distorting the gospel. And a distorted gospel is a false gospel. The true gospel of Jesus offers salvation by grace alone through faith alone.

Interestingly, this gospel issue is the same one that split the church during the Reformation in the sixteenth century. And we see the same problem today. Ultimately, if we try to add anything to the requirements for salvation—even with good intentions—what we're preaching is no longer the gospel of Christ. And in fact, it separates us from Christ (Galatians 5:4).

With that background and context in mind, let's see what we can learn from Paul's letter to the churches in Galatia.

WEEK 1

Galatians 1

Scripture to Memorize

You were called to freedom, brothers. Only do not use your freedom as an opportunity for the flesh, but through love serve one another.

Galatians 5:13

Note: If you haven't yet read How to Use This Study on page 7, please do that before continuing. It will provide you with a proper framework and helpful tools.

DAILY BIBLE READING

Day 1: Galatians 1:1–2

Day 2: Galatians 1:3–5

Day 3: Galatians 1:6–10

Day 4: Galatians 1:11–17

Day 5: Galatians 1:18–24

Day 6: Psalm 139

Day 7: Catch-Up Day

Corresponds to Day 328 of *The Bible Recap*.

WEEKLY CHALLENGE

See page 34 for more information.

DAY 1

Galatians 1:1–2

READ GALATIANS 1:1–2

We tend to speed past the greetings and salutations in many of the New Testament letters, but today we'll intentionally stop, park, and take in the scenery of the first two verses of Galatians. This brief passage is chock-full of foundational theology that will impact our view of the rest of the letter.

Review 1:1a.

Before we learn anything else about this letter to the Galatians, we find out who the writer is. It's widely accepted that Paul penned this letter, but acknowledging his authorship is only one important part of his opening sentence.

1. What one-word title did Paul use to describe himself in 1:1?

If you've never studied this term, you may not be familiar with the weight it carried for Paul's audience—or the weight it still carries for us today. It may seem like this title is interchangeable with *disciple*, but that's not the case.

2. **Using a Bible study tool, such as a Bible dictionary or encyclopedia, label the word clouds below.** Fill in the correct blank with the word "apostle" or "disciple."

BELIEVER

Teaches others

Learner ________________ STUDENT

FOLLOWER OF JESUS

Servant

Carried authority of God

Appointed by God

LEARNER Student

Servant ________________ Believer

WITNESS OF RESURRECTED CHRIST

Follower of Jesus

Review 1:1b.

In the early church, every apostle was a disciple, but not every disciple was an apostle. While the Bible speaks of many disciples of Jesus (Acts 6:1), and Jesus commissioned all believers to go make more disciples (Matthew 28:19–20), the office of apostle in the early church appears to be distinct. An apostle had to meet specific standards (Acts 1:21–22) and was appointed by God Himself to be a messenger and ambassador on His behalf.

Some people believe that the more general role of an apostle ("one who is sent out"[1]) still exists today. Others believe this was a position held by only those who met the qualifications above and no longer exists today.

★ 3. Why was Paul's title of apostle an important qualifier for those reading and hearing the letter?

★ 4. As we move forward in this study, why is it important for you to remember Paul's authority as a messenger of Christ even today?

Review 1:1b (one more time).

5. True or false: Jesus was alive when He called Paul to the ministry of apostleship?

A. True
B. False

The same God who commissioned Paul to be an apostle also raised Jesus from the dead. It can be easy to breeze past verses like these if you've heard the message dozens of times—especially if you've grown up in church. You may not remember a time when you *didn't know* God raised Jesus from the dead. But stop to ponder the miracle this is. Jesus was truly dead and in the grave. But by God's power and His plan, Jesus was raised on our behalf!

Review 1:2a.

The Greek word here for "brothers," translated from *adelphoi*, may refer to brothers or to brothers *and* sisters.[2] In this context, it was a reference to fellow believers and members of the family of God. As we'll see, it was important that the churches in Galatia not only understood Paul's level of authority, but also knew there were other believers standing behind him.

Review 1:2b.

The worldwide map below shows us where Galatia (modern-day Turkey) was located. As you read in the introduction, it's uncertain which portion of Galatia Paul originally wrote this letter to—northern Galatia or southern Galatia. Regardless, it was intended to be circulated to more than one group of people.

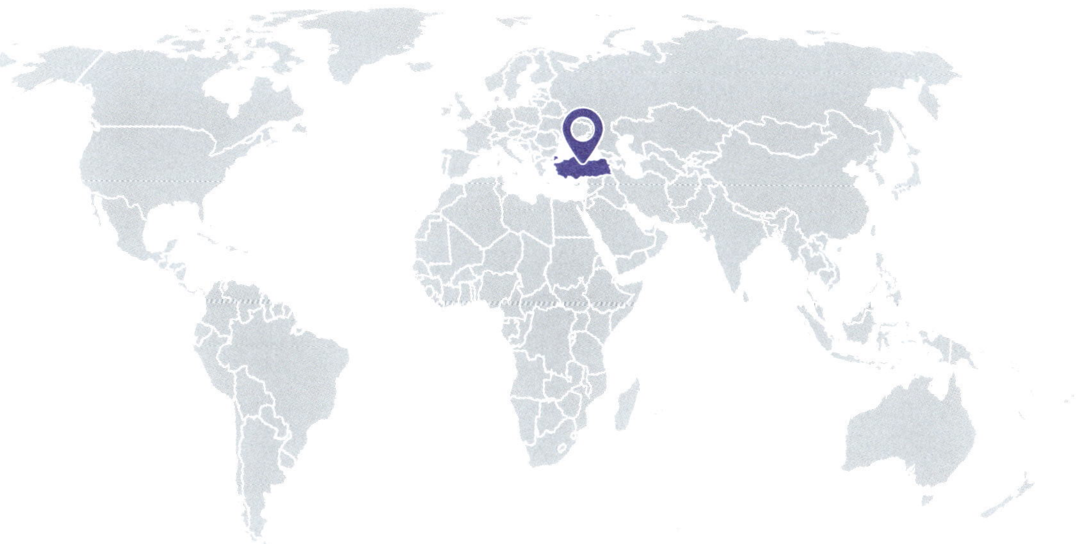

6. Draw a dotted line from the pin to wherever you're reading this letter today.

Paul likely never imagined his letter to the Galatians would travel the world with the message of grace—but God did. And it appears that God's Word "achieved the purpose for which it was sent" (see Isaiah 55:11 NIV).

DAY 2

Galatians 1:3–5

As Paul greeted the churches in Galatia, he led with a word that became the hallmark of his entire ministry.

Review 1:3.

Paul always wanted his readers to be reminded of grace. In fact, every one of Paul's letters begins with an extension of grace to his readers. He used this word more than one hundred times throughout his letters—nearly double the number of times it's used by other New Testament writers.[1]

1. Where do the grace and peace Paul speaks of originate?

2. How are the grace and peace of Jesus different from man's?

While this greeting of grace was common for Paul, this message was especially pertinent to the pickle the Galatians found themselves in. Before he laid out his argument to the churches and their infiltrators, he first laid out the good news.

Review 1:4a.

3. According to this verse, what two actions did Jesus perform on our behalf?

The first action is what theologians refer to as *substitutionary atonement*. The importance of this action can't be overstated. It was essential that the Galatians understood what took place for them on the cross, and it's crucial for us as well.

Breaking this down, *to substitute* means "to replace." *To atone* means "to make amends." Paul summarized the gospel at the beginning of the letter to explain that Jesus took our place when He died on the cross. And by taking our place, He took the death penalty we deserved because of our sins, making amends with God on our behalf. Most importantly, this atonement required nothing from us.

The second action, our deliverance from this present evil age, gave the Galatians hope. As we'll see in the pages to come, this was a very troubled and confused body of believers. Paul wanted to assure them that Jesus's work on their behalf had not stopped at the cross. They no longer had to be slaves of the world and its empty practices.

★ 4. What does deliverance from being a slave of this world mean to you? How does that give you hope when you're threatened by discouragement?

Review 1:4b.

Perhaps the most astonishing aspect of the entire gospel message is that God saves and delivers us because it's His will as our Father. In other words, He saves us *because He wants to*. Jesus willingly removed our sin through His death. And to that, there is only one response.

Review 1:5.

5. What do you think it means to give someone glory? Think of an athlete or celebrity—how have you seen that person glorified?

★ 6. How can we practically and actively attribute glory to Christ for what He has done for us?

Though the verse and section breaks in our Bibles weren't assigned by the original authors, take the break in this section to praise Jesus for what He's done. Give glory where glory is due. Bask in the grace and peace Paul has just extended. Because when we pick up in 1:6 tomorrow, we'll find that (to put it mildly) Paul was done with the pleasantries.

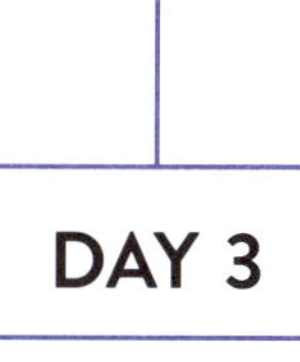

Galatians 1:6–10

READ GALATIANS 1:6–10

Paul's tone took a hard left turn in 1:6. This is a very different introduction from what you may be used to seeing in some of Paul's other letters. Instead of thanksgiving and praise for their growth and faithfulness, the Galatians received a sharp rebuke.

Review 1:6–7.

1. What was happening in the churches of Galatia that astonished Paul?

This is the first mention of the word *gospel* in Paul's letter. In fact, the word is used four times in just four verses. If you've grown up in church or you've followed Christ for a long time, it may be easy to throw the word *gospel* around, applying it to anything remotely related to church or Scripture. But without a solid understanding of its meaning, we're in danger of becoming like the Galatians and falling prey to those who distort it.

So what is the gospel?

2. **Using a Bible study tool, such as a Bible dictionary, briefly define *gospel* in the space below.** (We're not explaining the gospel message; we're simply defining the word itself.)

★ 3. Read Ephesians 2:8–9, then list everything about this message that sounds like good news to you.

4. According to these verses, what is God's role in salvation?

This is the true gospel—the "gospel of Christ" as Paul clarified in 1:7. Faith leads to salvation by God's grace and the finished work of Jesus, not by our works. The gospel is what God did for us, not what we do for Him. The gospel is *not* details about how to live a godly life—those are important things for us to know and they certainly glorify God, but that is our *response* to the gospel, not the gospel itself.

There were those among the Galatian churches who "troubled" the believers by "distorting" the gospel to the point where it was no longer the gospel at all—it was not good news. Later, we'll learn more of the specifics on exactly how these troublemakers (a group known as the Judaizers) were leading the Galatians astray, but we know simply by Paul's language that this distortion of the truth was something he took very seriously. At a minimum, it disrupted the peace the believers should've enjoyed—the peace that comes from resting in God's grace.

★ 5. Who or what "troubles" you or keeps you from resting in God's grace? Is it guilt, shame, feelings of unworthiness? Has someone made you think there's more you need to do to be in good standing with God?

Review 1:8–9.

Paul wasn't playing around. Any message or messenger—even an angel or Paul himself—who strays from what Jesus revealed as the path to salvation should be "accursed." He wasn't suggesting that the Galatians mildly shrug these teachers off and ignore them. He implored the believers to cut these so-called teachers off from the church and let God's wrath be upon them. For emphasis, Paul doubled down through repetition: "*Louder this time for the people in the back! Let. Him. Be. Accursed!*"

Review 1:10.

6. According to this verse, what threatens our purpose as servants of Christ?

The Judaizers likely tried to weaken Paul's influence over the Galatians. Religious zealots that they were, it's possible they accused him of watering down the gospel and building seeker-friendly churches in Galatia. But the commentary from the peanut gallery wasn't enough to deter Paul. He was now a servant of God. The approval of the Judaizers or any other religious leader did nothing for him anymore.

As we'll see in the next section, Paul was a changed man—and it was all because of God's grace. God had granted Paul the repentance and faith that led to his salvation. And now, empowered by the Spirit, he would faithfully proclaim the true gospel, come what may.

DAY 4

Galatians 1:11–17

READ GALATIANS 1:11–17

Review 1:11–12.

Paul continued to explain why it wasn't man's approval he was seeking as he preached the gospel: because the gospel he preached did not come from man. Sure, Paul saw value in man proclaiming the gospel—he himself was a preacher! But the Galatian churches were having trouble sifting through who was right and who was wrong. Did the Judaizers have the truth, or should they stick with Paul? The answer to this question was pivotal for the future of the church. Paul needed them to understand the divine source of his message.

1. How was the gospel revealed to Paul?

Review 1:13–14.

By sharing his testimony, how zealous he had been for Judaism, and how he'd persecuted the church of God, Paul pulled back the curtain on just how unfit he should be for preaching about Jesus.

2. Fill in the blanks in 1:14 below.

"... so extremely zealous was I for the traditions ____ ____ __________."

We know that Paul was a respected Pharisee, a "Hebrew of Hebrews" (Philippians 3:5). But the man-made traditions the Pharisees so strictly adhered to had carried them away from a sincere heart of devotion to God. In fact, it caused many of them to miss the gospel altogether. Before he came to Christ, Paul hadn't been zealous for faith or even zealous for a love for God. He was zealous for keeping a host of *man-made practices*. So now he, perhaps more than anyone, knew the danger this misguided zeal was to these young Galatian churches.

Review 1:15–16.

3. When did God set Paul apart?

A. When He felt like it

B. After Paul graduated from Pharisee school

C. Before Paul was born

D. When Paul proved himself good enough

★ 4. What does this tell you about God's sovereign plan for Paul's life?

It's hard for us, removed from the actual scene, to comprehend just how much the early church suffered at the hands of men who claimed to be religious—men like Paul. But this is the grace of God—that while Paul was spitting insults at Christians, dragging them to prison, and approving of their execution, God was *pleased* to save him.

5. According to 1:16, why did God reveal Jesus to Paul?

What must this have meant to a Gentile audience, to know that the God of the universe had a plan in place not only to save Paul, but to save Paul *so that* he would take the gospel to them? What a gift!

Review 1:17.

It might have made more sense for Paul to go to Jerusalem after God placed this calling on his life. After all, it was a ministry hub for many of the other apostles. But Paul wanted to make sure his audience knew that the message he had preached to them was not received from any man (see 1:12). Plus, Jerusalem's population was primarily Jewish, and Paul was called to the Gentiles. So he eventually returned to Damascus.

★ 6. Read Acts 9:1–2. How was Paul's mission to Damascus different this time around?

Paul's life is a testimony to the powerlessness of man's religious traditions—and to the life-changing power of grace.

DAY 5

Galatians 1:18–24

READ GALATIANS 1:18–24

This week concludes with Paul describing the timeline of his ministry following his conversion. For further study, Acts 9:19–31 provides Luke's description of this time in Paul's life. However, in the context of this letter, Paul wasn't simply giving an autobiography; he was guiding his audience toward an essential point in his story.

Review 1:18–20.

1. On the map below, circle where Paul went following his conversion (see the end of 1:17), and note on the map how long he stayed there.

Just as the twelve disciples spent three years learning from Jesus during His earthly ministry, Paul also had the opportunity to continue learning from the Lord as he spent three years in obscurity. It's important to remember that Paul's life had just been turned upside down. Everything he'd wholeheartedly believed had been refuted by the Lord Himself, and because of that, he'd gone from being a celebrated religious elite to being the bane of the Pharisees' existence. It's likely that those three years were spent in fellowship and prayer as his commission to the Gentiles was confirmed.

★ 2. Do you remember what it was like when you first believed in Jesus? How did it change the way you lived, thought, and spoke? Did those changes happen immediately, or did they take time?

3. Go back to the map on the previous page and draw a dotted line from Damascus to the place Paul said he traveled to next. Note on the map how long he was there.

It may feel a bit confusing that Paul said he was going "up" to Jerusalem when Jerusalem is south of Damascus. But Jerusalem is located in the mountains, so it was "up" no matter where a person was traveling from.

While in Jerusalem, Paul visited with Peter and James. (If your Bible translation uses the name Cephas, this is simply the Aramaic name for Peter; you'll continue to see these names used interchangeably throughout the letter.) As Paul recounted his visit with these two leaders of the church, he was quick to tell the Galatians that they were the only apostles he saw, and even this was only for a short visit.

As one commentary notes, "Paul showed that there was *enough* contact between him and the other apostles to show that they were in perfect agreement, but *not so much* that it showed that Paul got his gospel from them instead of God."[1]

Review 1:21–23.

4. Using a solid line or a different color, mark the map on page 28 to show where Paul went next.

Acts 9:29–30 says he went there because the Jews in Jerusalem were plotting to kill him. But this didn't stop God's plan and the ripple effect of Paul's testimony.

Though the Judeans didn't know Paul personally, his reputation certainly preceded him. Up to this point, believers had been scattered all over the region, running for their lives because of Paul and his power-hungry, bloodthirsty religious cohorts.

But now a new reputation was spreading about him. His zeal had been redirected, and he was a man on a mission. No longer a mission to persecute but to preach. No longer filled with hatred but filled with the Spirit of God. No longer a man to fear, but an example to follow.

★ 5. Ask a friend or mentor what they've noticed about the impact Christ has made on your life. Write what you learn.

Review 1:24.

While heaven rejoices when even one sinner repents (Luke 15:7), Paul's conversion was—without a doubt—a shock to the religious system of the day. For the Judaizers who were trying to undermine the gospel, this news must have been infuriating. But for the weary, persecuted Christians, it drove them to worship.

As Paul's new reputation spread through the Christian grapevine, the whispers might have sounded something like this: *"The man who hated followers of Christ has finally found what we've found—that He's where the joy is!"*

6. What stood out to you most in this week's study? Why?

7. What did you learn or relearn about God and His character this week?

DAY 6

Corresponding Psalm & Prayer

READ PSALM 139

1. What correlation do you see between Psalm 139 and this week's study?

2. What portions of this psalm stand out to you most?

3. Close by praying this prayer aloud:

Father,

You sent Jesus and You raised Him from the dead. Jesus, You gave Yourself for our sins to deliver us from the present evil age. Spirit, no matter where I go, You are there. Like David wrote, Your works are wonderful, and my soul knows it very well. Like Paul wrote, the glory forever and ever is Yours!

Search me, O God, and know my heart. With one breath, I praise You, and with the next, I sin against You. There are times when Paul's strong words to the Galatians should be directed at me. I have so quickly deserted You and turned to a false gospel—one that gives me credit for my own salvation. I repent, Lord.

Help me rest in Your grace. Remind me that grace and peace—and everything good, true, and holy—come from You alone. Help me to glorify You—the one who knit me together in my mother's womb. Every day, guide my actions, words, and thoughts so that they bring You glory.

I surrender my life to You, Lord—every moment of my day, each decision I make, I yield my will and way to Your perfect will and way.

I love You too. Amen.

DAY 7

Rest, Catch Up, or Dig Deeper

WEEKLY CHALLENGE

On Days 4 and 5 (in Galatians 1:13–24), Paul recounted a few elements of his conversion story and his call to ministry. While this wasn't his full testimony, he used a sampling of his faith journey to open his letter to the Galatians and support everything he was about to tell them.

Choosing to share part(s) of your faith journey is different from sharing the testimony of Christ's work in saving you. The practice Paul modeled in these verses is a great tool! It provides an opportunity to begin a faith conversation with someone—or you can use it as an on-ramp to share the gospel.

Choose an aspect of your story that might resonate with someone who isn't a believer in Jesus. Write out a few ways you might use that story to segue into a spiritual conversation or a gospel-sharing opportunity.

WEEK 2

Galatians 2

Scripture to Memorize

For the whole law is fulfilled in one word: "You shall love your neighbor as yourself."

Galatians 5:14

DAILY BIBLE READING

Day 1: Galatians 2:1–5

Day 2: Galatians 2:6–10

Day 3: Galatians 2:11–14

Day 4: Galatians 2:15–16

Day 5: Galatians 2:17–21

Day 6: Psalm 143

Day 7: Catch-Up Day

Corresponds to Day 328 of *The Bible Recap*.

WEEKLY CHALLENGE

See page 57 for more information.

DAY 1

Galatians 2:1–5

READ GALATIANS 2:1–5

Review 2:1–3.

In 1:18, Paul mentioned a trip he made to Jerusalem three years after his conversion. Here in 2:1, he described a second journey to Jerusalem fourteen years later, alongside Barnabas and Titus. This second trip is likely either the one when Paul and Barnabas delivered famine relief to Jewish Christians (Acts 11:27–30) or the one to the Jerusalem Council (Acts 15:1–31).

1. **Using an online research tool, determine which of the following best describes the Jerusalem Council.**

A. A yearly gathering of leading church members in Jerusalem
B. A meeting among Jewish Christian leadership (~AD 48–50) to establish official decisions about early church disagreements over whether Gentile converts were required to follow Jewish law
C. An amazing outdoor worship concert by the Sea of Galilee
D. A court case in AD 46 concerning the practice of sheep sacrifices

2. According to Acts 15:29, the Jerusalem Council determined only four requirements for Gentile converts in the early church. Draw an X over the item that was not on that list.

abstain from food sacrificed to idols   abstain from what has been strangled

abstain from blood   abstain from sexual immorality

be circumcised

The heart behind the verdict of the Jerusalem Council was for unity within the church—the ability for Jewish and Gentile Christians to eat together at tables. These rules were about maintaining peace, not about attaining salvation; after all, the gospel made it clear that salvation was by God's grace and Christ's finished work, not by man's works.

Because scholars aren't certain as to the exact date Galatians was written, they also can't be sure whether it was written before or after the Jerusalem Council. However, in either case, it's clear this debate about whether Gentile converts were required to follow Mosaic law was one that plagued the early church on more than one occasion. It was officially addressed and put to rest at the Jerusalem Council, and *still* it was necessary for Paul to address it and re-address it in many of his letters throughout the New Testament. And Paul's tone in this letter reveals that he was deeply burdened by the stumbling block the debate continued to present for those who were hearing and believing the gospel.

Barnabas, also known as Joses, was a Jewish Christian who was well-respected by the Jewish leadership. He was a Levite, which means he was of the priestly tribe of Israel. Conversely, Titus was a Gentile convert to Christianity. As it turns out, these two companions served to be a perfect microcosm of the issue at hand.

3. Why did Paul say he went to Jerusalem in 2:2?

Modern readers sometimes view Paul's language choices as harsh or perhaps even arrogant. But 2:2 is a great example of how he exhibited great humility, reserving his boldness for preaching the gospel. He didn't just receive a revelation from God and then go off on his own. He traveled to Jerusalem to submit to the authority there and make sure his revelation was in alignment with the gospel they were preaching.

He reminded his readers that on that specific trip, the Jewish leadership had not required Titus the Greek Gentile Christian to be circumcised. But because of *pseudadelphos* ("false brothers"), they were suddenly changing their tune—not because of a revelation from God, but because of false teaching.

Review 2:4–5.

4. The language in 2:4–5 is a great example of Paul's humility contrasted with his unyielding boldness for the gospel. On the left, note words from this passage that hint at his humble stance. On the right, note the language that conveys his gospel boldness. (Hint: Bear in mind that Paul was already circumcised when he wrote this letter.)

Humility	Boldness

★ 5. Describe a scenario in your own life where you might have the opportunity to exhibit humility alongside gospel boldness.

★ 6. Do you find it difficult to distinguish between the two? If so, describe.

Paul was a "Hebrew of Hebrews" (Philippians 3:5), highly educated in the most well-respected circles of Judaism before his conversion to Christianity. But Paul counted all this as loss (Philippians 3:8) and identified himself with the lowly, with the Gentiles to whom he was called, with the uncircumcised "that the truth of the gospel might be preserved for you" (Galatians 2:5).

He wrote this letter to the Galatians. But as it is the inspired Word of God, may we receive it today.

7. Finish 2:5 with your own name.

"... that the truth of the gospel might be preserved for ______________."

DAY 2

Galatians 2:6–10

READ GALATIANS 2:6–10

Review 2:6.

In today's reading, Paul finished his story about the Jerusalem trip, reminding his audience of what was clearly established before he left. By saying that the influential leaders of the Jerusalem church "added nothing to me," he meant they were affirming that his understanding of the gospel was accurate. The personal revelation he received didn't require correction from them.

Review 2:7–9.

The leaders expressed that they were in full alignment with Paul's calling. Paul's purpose in mentioning the influential wasn't to borrow fame or participate in celebrity culture. Popular teachers and leaders of that time were just as susceptible to receiving or desiring improper attention as they are now. And Paul always went out of his way to maintain that God gets the glory (1:5). But the influential are mentioned here to remind readers that even the influential not only agreed with him about this issue, but *doubled down* by endorsing it, recognizing the distinct callings they saw Paul and Peter had on their lives.

1. Referencing 2:7–8, draw lines to match the apostle to the people group he ministered to.

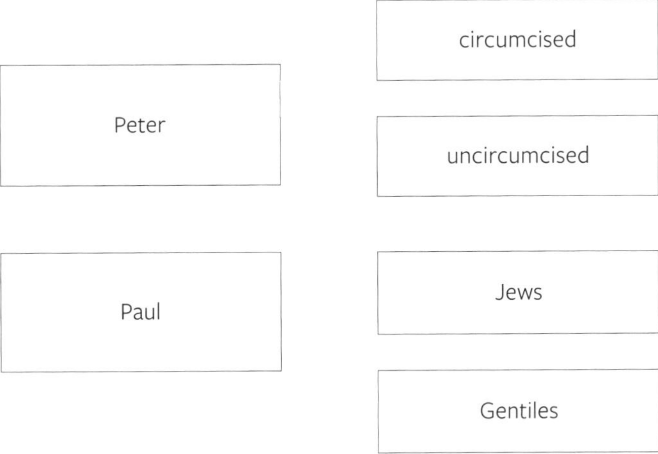

2. According to 2:8, who empowered both in their ministries?

This isn't to say that from that point on, Paul never ministered to Jews again and Peter never ministered to Gentiles. By no means. For example, someone who spent most of their life as a missionary in France wouldn't hesitate to share the gospel with someone they came across in Boston just because they were called to be a missionary to France. That wasn't the point. The point was they'd already established both circumcised and uncircumcised people groups as legitimate and separate groups that would be ministered to as part of one unified church. This church would be made up of both circumcised and uncircumcised believers. And it was God who had laid those callings on their hearts.

Peter, James, and John—pillars of the Jerusalem church—were in complete alignment with Paul's calling to the uncircumcised, just as they saw Peter was called to the circumcised. They'd even sealed it with a handshake.

Review 2:10.

3. What was the only thing these pillars of the church asked of Paul?

4. What was Paul's response to that?

The poor referred to in this passage were likely Jewish Christians being persecuted in Jerusalem. Throughout his ministry, Paul put a lot of effort into encouraging the Gentile Christian churches to gather and send financial aid to their Jewish Christian brothers and sisters in Jerusalem. There was no sense of defiance in their distinctness, no sense of "*Hey, we're new, and we're Gentiles, so we don't have to consider you Jews, and we'll do whatever we want.*" There was great care and consideration, a unity of heart that completely defied the norms of the day.

★ 5. What kind of impact do you think it would've had on the spread of the gospel for unbelievers to see circumcised and uncircumcised Christians taking care of one another in this way, in this culture?

★ 6. Have you been a recipient of or participant in this kind of care across distinct people groups? If so, describe. Did you notice a sense of unity through Christ that perhaps wasn't there before?

Paul's trip to Jerusalem ended in absolute alignment and unity—full stop. He went to great lengths to emphasize this because of what happened in tomorrow's passage. Stay tuned!

DAY 3

Galatians 2:11–14

Review 2:11–12.

Our study on Day 2 ended with the facts firmly established: During the trip Paul, Barnabas, and Titus took to Jerusalem, the church was unified in full alignment concerning circumcised and uncircumcised Christians.

Today's study finds them seated at separate tables. Imagine the scene: the Christians at Antioch perhaps excitedly anticipating the great disciple Peter's arrival at their home church. But when "certain men . . . from James" arrived—and after all that had been established in Jerusalem—Peter essentially said to the Gentile Christians, "*You can't sit with us.*"

We don't know for sure who these "certain men" were, but we can assume they were intimidating or powerful in some way, perhaps influential Judaizers. Whatever the case, Peter seemed to be threatened by them. There was an inconsistency between what he believed and how he behaved—thus in the court of logic he "stood condemned."

★ 1. Who are your "certain men from James"? What are the environments where, because of fear of man, you find yourself quick to abandon the things you know to be true?

Review 2:13.

The Greek word for "hypocrite" here refers to an actor. It means "one who puts on a mask." Peter and the rest of the Jews present knew the Gentile believers were truly Christians, but because of their own fears, they acted like they didn't. And even Paul's traveling companion Barnabas, whose nickname among the apostles was Son of Encouragement (Acts 4:36), followed suit.

2. In this situation, how might Barnabas more aptly be nicknamed?

A. Son of Double Encouragement
B. Son of No Worries—It's Not That Big of a Deal
C. Son of Discouragement

Considering Peter was the leader of this disheartening step backward, it was especially disconcerting. It was Peter who'd first received the direct revelation from God concerning Jewish Christians dining with Gentiles (Acts 10:1–11:18). In short, God said, *"Do it."*

There may have been other Jewish Christians who still earnestly had concerns about needing to follow Mosaic law, even though they were now also Christians. But Peter knew better, and Paul made clear that it was only because of the fear of man that he was saying otherwise. There wasn't a doctrine change—Peter didn't have a new revelation from God. He'd just fallen back into old fears.

If you're familiar with the story of Jesus's crucifixion, this may sound familiar. Peter—who'd literally walked with Jesus on land and on water, who was the first to declare the divinity of Christ (Matthew 16:16–17)—*that* Peter denied the truth three times during Jesus's arrest. And here in 2:12, we see it happened all over again.

On the one hand, this serves as an important reminder that there's no spiritual celebrity status here on earth in which we become unable to sin. Praise God our salvation is by faith alone.

But on the other hand, this story is of great encouragement. In Matthew 26:34, Jesus predicted that before the rooster crowed three times, Peter would deny Him. Jesus knew Peter would deny Him, and Jesus knew Peter would deny the truth again here. Yet He still chose him to feed His sheep (see John 21:15–17).

3. Write the word *never* in all caps in the blanks below, and praise God that it's true!

We're ________ too great to mess up. And we've ________ messed up God's ability to work all things for our good and His glory. (See Romans 8:28.)

Case in point: God is likely using Peter's story to encourage *you* in light of your own failures, even today.

★ 4. Do you struggle to believe this is true? Describe an area of your life (past or present) in which you struggle to believe that God is able to work things for His glory and your good.

5. What biblical truths can you pray over your heart and that situation? What are some scripturally based worship songs you can sing when doubt creeps in?

Review 2:14.

Because of the revelation Peter had received about Jewish Christians communing with Gentiles (Acts 10:1–11:18), Peter wasn't even keeping the Mosaic law anymore. So Paul pointed out that he had no grounds on which to force the Gentiles to keep it.

6. Draw a line from any works in the left column that produce our salvation.

Jesus's saving work on the cross	Salvation
Circumcision	
Mosaic law	
Our good deeds	

DAY 4

Galatians 2:15–16

READ GALATIANS 2:15–16

Review 2:15.

Today's passage builds on what Paul said to Peter at Antioch. He unpacked the essence of his argument to help his readers understand why he confronted Peter *and* why it was important. This wasn't an issue of petty drama between two famous church leaders. This was a matter of reiterating and clarifying the gospel.

1. Who did the "we" in 2:15 refer to?

Peter was, by birth, a Jew, but also a lowly fisherman. He probably wasn't highly educated. Paul, also born a Jew, was, as we discussed on Day 1 of this week, a "Hebrew of Hebrews" (Philippians 3:5). He was educated by the best of the best, was raised as an expert in the Mosaic law, and was likely from a wealthy or influential family. And yet, he referred to himself and Peter as "we." Amid this public correction of Peter, notice the great sense of humility Paul embeds in this "we" statement.

In this ancient culture, two men of such disparate social standing in Judaism—prior to their conversions to Christianity—wouldn't necessarily be grouped in a "we" statement by the superior party. But the point was that whether one of them was a lowly Jewish fisherman or the most law-abiding of all Jews, it didn't matter—that status still didn't bring salvation. Neither their birth nor their observance of the law brought salvation. "For it is impossible for the blood of bulls and goats to take away sins" (see Hebrews 10:1–4).

The term "Gentile sinners" referred to people who weren't Jewish *and* who didn't know the one true God. But regardless of the way the Gentiles were referred to in this culture, Paul was making a point.

2. Bearing that in mind, of the two groups mentioned in 2:15, circle the sinners.

Jews by birth   Gentile sinners

Review 2:16.

"There is no one righteous, not even one" (Romans 3:10 NIV). Paul wrote that in his inspired letter to the Romans, and he was quoting Psalm 14. From the Old Testament to the New, from Jew to Gentile, from ancient times until the moment Paul confronted Peter, and even until now, there has been no one righteous but Jesus, who died to save us.

3. According to 2:16, who will be justified by works of the law?

4. Again, who did the "we" refer to in this verse?

Paul was getting personal with Peter: *"Peter, you know this! We also have believed, just as the Gentile sinners, in order to be justified by faith, not by works."*

This is the first time Paul used the word *justified* (ancient Greek: *dikaioō*) in his letter to the Galatians. If you've grown up around faith terminology, it's a word you may feel overly familiar with. It might be easy to miss the point. So lean in.

5. Fill in the blanks below with *I* to personalize your reading of this impactful statement on the justification we're offered in Christ.

> ". . . yet __ know that __ [am] not justified by works of the law but through faith in Jesus Christ . . ."

★ **6. Does this feel like good news to you when you read it aloud? Why or why not?**

Justification is a legal term. It refers to a verdict in a court of law. And God is not unjust. He doesn't ask for two payments for the same debt—that would be unjust. The great exchange we get with Jesus is like seeing a judge looking at our file in court, but rather than laying down the verdict that matches our file, the judge lays down the verdict according to Jesus's perfect file.

Though this is the best news we could ever hear, the powerful "certain men with James" might have considered this a lot to lose. Observant Jews put a lot of energy into keeping the law. Their whole lives revolved around it. And their keeping of it may have felt somewhat transactional in their hearts—a sense of security or earning their feeling of rightness before God.

To lose that would be something their flesh might object to—even as they were met with the truth that what was being offered to them in Christ was freedom from the law, freedom from striving, and an invitation into His perfect record being imputed to them.

★ 7. Is there any part of your heart that imagines feeling safer by striving for your own salvation through works, rather than embracing the truth that salvation cannot be earned? What truths from Galatians that you've learned so far might set you free from that kind of false thinking and striving?

DAY 5

Galatians 2:17–21

READ GALATIANS 2:17–21

Review 2:17.

In today's passage, Paul concluded his summary of his argument to Peter. As you dive in, it's important to note that Paul didn't hate the Mosaic law. In fact, he aimed to keep it. And he even went to great lengths to make vows and voluntarily deprive himself of certain pleasures or comforts for the sake of spreading the gospel (Acts 18:18). The key distinction Paul made here was that obeying the law isn't what saves us. The law was "but a shadow of the good things to come" (Hebrews 10:1).

That "thing to come" was Christ. And 2:17 emphasizes that our salvation comes from Christ's saving work on the cross, not our works. However, to continue to sin in order to somehow "prove" that our salvation comes not from works but from Christ is "certainly not" the endeavor. Christ isn't a servant of sin. The cause of Christ doesn't need the assistance of your sin to be made legitimate. As Paul wrote in Romans 6:1–2, "Are we to continue in sin that grace may abound? By no means!" Grace doesn't need you to do it a favor by continuing to sin to prove how great it is.

Review 2:18–20.

If your response to 2:18 was *Huh?* fear not. Let's unpack this. Paul was talking about the errors of legalism here. If you try to be *more* in right standing with God by adding requirements to salvation, that actually makes you *less* in right standing with Him. If Christ's saving work on the cross freed us from the Mosaic law, to suggest His work still needs our adherence to the Mosaic law makes us transgressors indeed.

1. True or false: In 2:19, Paul said the law died.

The law is what shows we need a Savior—it reveals God's holiness. It didn't die. But Paul said *he* died *to* it, because it's not the means of our rescue. It's just what shows us that we need rescue. "Through the law" Paul saw that he was incapable of saving himself by keeping it; thus he died to it so that he might live to God.

2. According to 2:20, the life Paul "now live[s] in the flesh" is lived by what?

    A. Faith in his ability to keep the law
    B. His ability to be like Christ
    C. Faith in the Son of God

"In the flesh" isn't referring to a fleshly or sinful way of thinking (which is often how the phrase is used in his other letters). In this passage, he's making the point that *right now*, in our bodies on earth, we get to live in Christ. Salvation isn't just a "ticket to heaven"—it's the catalyst for new life in Him, which includes the resurrection power we get to live in now.

3. Fill in the blanks in 2:20 below. Picture Paul writing the words as you do it.

"... the Son of God, who loved ____ and gave himself for ____."

Notice how personal that is! Paul knew Jesus died for him *personally*—even when Jesus knew Paul would persecute Him personally (Acts 9:4).

★ 4. What in your own life story makes this truth a comfort?

Review 2:21.

We don't know what Peter's immediate response was to Paul's correction. But when Paul suggested that thinking righteousness comes through the law "nullif[ies] the grace of God," we can wonder what Peter pictured. Peter had personally watched Jesus sweat blood in the garden of Gethsemane on the night before He died, asking the Father if there was any other way salvation might be accomplished.

But there was no other way. The cross was where salvation was. And because of His finished work on the cross, we get to know and love Him! He's where the joy is!

★ 5. What stood out to you most in this week's study? Why?

6. What did you learn or relearn about God and His character this week?

DAY 6

Corresponding Psalm & Prayer

READ PSALM 143

1. What correlation do you see between Psalm 143 and this week's study?

2. What portions of this psalm stand out to you most?

3. Close by praying this prayer aloud:

Father,

You are faithful and You are righteous, even when we are unfaithful and unrighteous. You are perfect, yet You use imperfect people to accomplish Your plans. Thank You for creating me, loving me, and using me for Your glory.

The truth of the gospel has been preserved for me, but like the Judaizers, I've made my own requirements for how my brothers and sisters should live. I've arrogantly made assumptions about their faith based on what they wear, what they eat or drink, or where they go. Like with Peter, there has been a disconnect between what I believe and how I've behaved. Instead of working to build unity in Your church, I've sowed division. Forgive me, God.

Like David wrote, let me hear in the morning of Your steadfast love. Make me know the way I should go. Show me how to work for unity with my brothers and sisters. And help us show the world that You are the great unifier.

I surrender my life to You, Lord—every moment of my day, each decision I make, I yield my will and way to Your perfect will and way.

I love You too. Amen.

DAY 7

Rest, Catch Up, or Dig Deeper

WEEKLY CHALLENGE

On Day 5, Paul corrected the lie that grace equals freedom to sin. Thinking of sin as something we're "free" to do would be a huge misunderstanding of the nature of sin and how it affects the quality of our lives. As Jesus said in John 8:34, sin isn't freedom—sin is slavery. Have you ever been tricked into thinking of sin as a kind of freedom you miss out on as a Christian?

On a piece of paper, draw a bottle of poison. On your drawing, write a few particularly tempting sins that tend to masquerade as freedom in your heart and mind. In your journal, write a prayer asking God to help you remember the truth about the nature of sin and its effects (and repent where necessary). Then safely burn or destroy the paper with your drawing.

WEEK 3

Galatians 3

Scripture to Memorize

But if you bite and devour one another, watch out that you are not consumed by one another.

Galatians 5:15

DAILY BIBLE READING

Day 1: Galatians 3:1–9
Day 2: Galatians 3:10–14
Day 3: Galatians 3:15–18
Day 4: Galatians 3:19–22
Day 5: Galatians 3:23–29
Day 6: Psalm 19
Day 7: Catch-Up Day

Corresponds to Day 328 of *The Bible Recap*.

WEEKLY CHALLENGE

See page 81 for more information.

DAY 1

Galatians 3:1–9

The Galatians had fallen for false teaching, believing that salvation was dependent on their own works. Paul set the record straight, reminding them of the truth and beauty of the gospel.

Review 3:1.

Without mincing words, Paul insisted that they had once understood the gospel so clearly that it had been as if they were there in Jerusalem, watching with their own eyes when Jesus died for them. And yet somehow, Paul pointed out, they had twisted Jesus's sacrificial love into something they must earn. So Paul wrote harshly, calling the Galatians foolish—not because he didn't love them, but because he *did* love them and because truly understanding the gospel is a matter of life and death.

Review 3:2–5.

Speaking to their reality as Gentile Christians, Paul asked the Galatians "only this." (Okay, he actually asked five questions, but who's counting?) This series of questions reminded them of what was true about their faith.

By scaffolding questions, Paul built his case: It's absurd and heretical to insist that salvation is earned. Let's unpack Paul's questions and build his case with him.

1. Circle the correct answer to each question below.

How did the Gentile Christians in Galatia receive the Spirit?

By works of the law — By hearing with faith

Are they really that foolish?

Yes — No — Hard to say

How were they being perfected?

By the flesh — By the Spirit

When they suffered because of their faith, was it worthless?

Yes, it was all in vain — No, it had a purpose

Why did God give them the Spirit and work miracles among them?

Because they obeyed the law — Because they heard with faith

Like a devoted teacher unapologetically guiding his students back to the truth, Paul reminded the Galatians of what they once knew: *"It is by God's grace that you have been justified before Him, and it is by God's grace that you are being sanctified to be more like Him."*

Review 3:6.

Having reminded them of their experiences as Gentile Christians, Paul continued to build his case in defense of the truth of the gospel. Now he used Scripture itself—the law and the patriarchs that the Judaizers claimed to love so much.

According to *Enduring Word*'s commentary, ancient rabbis praised Abraham for keeping the law and held him up as an example of obedience. So the Judaizers might have been surprised to hear Paul hold Abraham up as an example of *faith*.[1]

2. Find the mistake in the sentence below, crossing out the word that shouldn't be there. Use 3:6 as your guide.

Abraham believed in God, and it was counted to him as righteousness.

3. Why does that word make such a difference here?

Abraham's belief was counted to him as righteousness, which shows us that there is an element of human responsibility here. What we do certainly matters—we must take action. Sometimes that action is with our hands and feet, and sometimes that action is in our hearts and minds. And still, our action is ignited by, enabled by, and in response to God.

Abraham believed God; he believed that His character was perfect, His goodness was real, His grace was sufficient, and His promise was true. And Abraham's belief was made possible by the perfect, real, sufficient, and true grace of God.

Review 3:7.

Since the Galatians were capable of understanding and believing all that Paul was saying, he was confident that they would also know this: "It is those of faith who are the sons of Abraham."

4. Read Genesis 12:1–3 and Luke 19:9. Who are the "sons of Abraham"?

★ 5. What did this mean for the Galatians?

★ 6. What does it mean for you?

There have been times throughout history when 3:7 has been taken out of context to justify truly horrific persecution of Jewish people. But in the rightful context of this letter, and in the wider context of Scripture as a whole, we understand its meaning: Though God had, and has, a special covenant relationship with ethnic Israel, His plan was always to extend His covenant to include Gentiles (see also Romans 11, Genesis 18, and Deuteronomy 30).

Review 3:8–9.

God made a covenant with Abraham *before* He gave His people the law. The promise came first. The gospel was there all along: *The Savior was coming.* And through Him, the promise would be fulfilled.

The gospel isn't a bait-and-switch scam; it doesn't invite people into faith only to make them strive to earn or keep it. Nothing the Galatians had ever done—or would ever do—could render them able to earn or perfect their salvation. Nothing you've ever done—or will ever do—can render you able to earn or perfect your salvation.

Just as it invites us today, the gospel invited the Galatians to have faith in Jesus's perfect works, to receive the Father's priceless gift, and to trust in the Spirit's faultless guidance. *He does the doing*, and aren't you so glad He does?

DAY 2

Galatians 3:10–14

Still building a case, Paul continued pointing to Scripture in defense of the gospel. And when he pointed to Scripture to make a case, he was *thorough*. Quoting at least one Old Testament passage in each verse of this section, he meticulously crafted a gospel presentation.

Drawing on the Old Testament to teach the gospel was a tactic he often employed when he wrote to Jewish Christians. While it's true that the Galatian Christians were mostly Gentile converts, many scholars agree that there were some Jewish Christians among their numbers. Perhaps Paul also thought, or even hoped, that the Judaizers who had led the Galatians astray would read his letter. Whatever his intentions, he used the Scriptures—the very same Scriptures that the Judaizers claimed to hold in such high esteem—to teach the gospel.

Review 3:10–14.

★ 1. For each row in the table below, review the verse listed from Galatians, then read the Old Testament passage Paul quoted there. Finally, summarize each verse of his teaching in your own words.

Review	Read the Quoted Verse(s)	Summarize Paul's Teaching
3:10	Deuteronomy 27:26	
3:11	Habakkuk 2:4	

3:12	Leviticus 18:5	
3:13	Deuteronomy 21:23	
3:14	Isaiah 32:15; 44:3	

Working through Scripture, Paul pointed out that anyone who failed to keep the law was cursed, deserving death. Of course, that meant *all* of the Galatians who might read his letter—Gentiles, Jews, and Judaizers—deserved death. But because Jesus became the curse—dying a humiliating, agonizing death, even after He'd lived a perfect, law-abiding life—those who believed were made righteous. And marking them as His own, God gave them a seal: the Holy Spirit.

Just as the Galatians were reminded of the gospel here, let this be our reminder too: Jesus not only saved us from the death we deserve, but also gave us the blessing we could never earn. Theologians call this the Great Exchange. That blessing includes the gift of the Holy Spirit. God sent His Spirit to live in every believer as a seal of our salvation and also to serve us in many other ways, including as our teacher, guide, helper, and comforter (John 14:26; John 16:13; Romans 8:26–27; John 14:16–17).

★ 2. Keeping the list above in mind, in what ways has the Holy Spirit worked in your life lately? Be specific.

3. Write a prayer of gratitude thanking God for the blessing of the Spirit's presence and for His work in your life.

DAY 3

Galatians 3:15–18

READ GALATIANS 3:15–18

Paul previously argued that true understanding of the gospel was proven by the reality of the Galatians' experience as Gentile believers. And he'd argued that true understanding of the gospel was proven by Scripture itself. But he wasn't finished arguing.

Review 3:15.

With the single Greek word *adelphos*—which many English translations record as "brothers and sisters"—he reminded the believers that even though he rebuked them for their wandering hearts and foolish beliefs, they were still his brothers and sisters. Which meant, of course, they were also Jesus's brothers and sisters. So here, Paul reminded his family that the gospel is true with one more argument.

1. In the third column in the drawing on the next page, write the gist of Paul's third argument, which proves the true gospel.

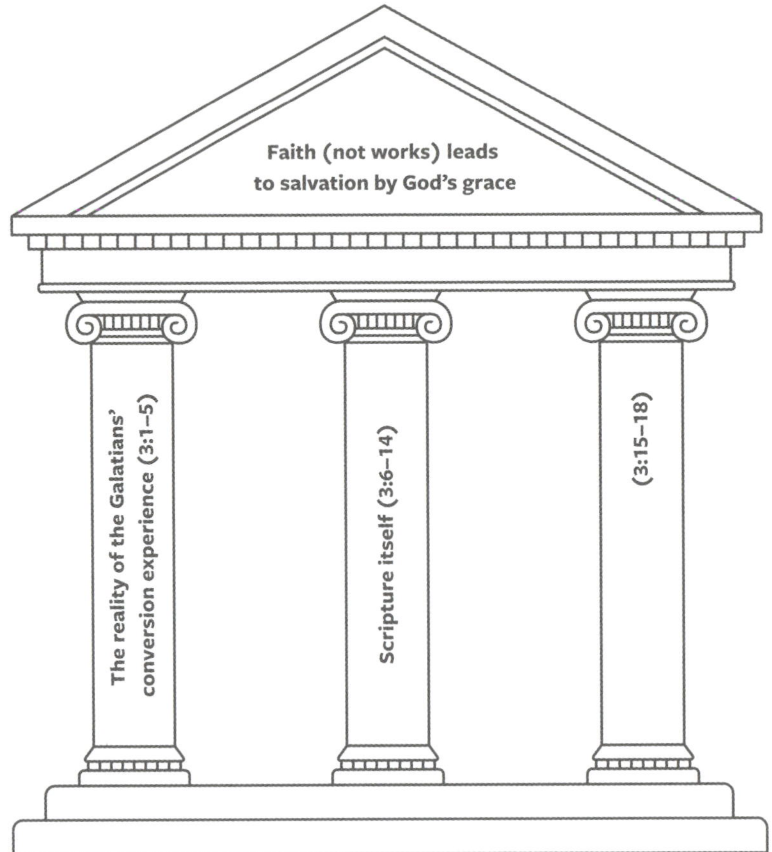

Covenant, or *diathēkē* in Greek, was the same word people used at that time to describe a legal will, one that dictated the distribution of property and possessions after death. Like they do today, this type of will dictated who heirs were and what their inheritance was. These covenants were binding, which meant that once they were ratified (or formally approved), they couldn't be subtracted from, added to, or voided. And if the Galatians understood *that*, Paul argued, then they also understood the gospel as proven through God's covenant.

Review 3:16–17.

2. Read the verses below. Who did God say would dwell in the land?

Genesis 13:15—

Genesis 17:8—

While it's true that Abraham's descendants were as numerous as the stars—just as God had promised they would be—the truest, most complete fulfillment of God's promises to Abraham is the one singular offspring, Jesus Christ. And through Him, *all* of God's kids (people whom He has adopted into His family) are made righteous (Romans 5:19). God was always going to send His Son, and He made that promise 430 years before He gave the law.

If you're one of the three people out there checking Paul's math, there are a few thoughts on where this number came from. A common theory is based on a Septuagint translation of Exodus 12:40, which marks the time from Abraham to the Israelites' exodus from Egypt. Others believe this marks the time between God's confirmation of His promise to Jacob before he went to Egypt (Genesis 46:3–4) and when the law was given to Moses (Exodus 20).[1]

But no matter where the countdown started or ended, the point is the same: The law did not void the promise. The promise was ratified—formally approved—by God Himself first. So His covenant was binding, which meant that it could never be subtracted from, added to, or voided.

Review 3:18.

Just like in a legal will, God's covenant—His unchangeable promise—has heirs and an inheritance. If that inheritance was contingent on obedience to the law, there would be only one heir: Jesus. But as Paul wrote in another letter, all Christ-followers are "heirs—heirs of God and co-heirs with Christ" (Romans 8:17 NIV).

So what is this promised inheritance? At the time this was written, the promised land had already been in and out of ethnic Israel's possession many times—and that's still happening today. So thank God the inheritance He promised is so much more than just the land!

3. Read each passage below and write how our inheritance is described.

Romans 8:17—

2 Corinthians 4:17—

1 Peter 1:4—

Revelation 21:4—

The Galatian Christians were co-heirs to this inheritance. The promise came first, and even when they failed to keep God's laws, His promise could not be subtracted from, added to, or voided. If you are in Christ, *you* are a co-heir to this inheritance. The promise came first, and even when you fail to keep God's laws, His promise cannot be subtracted from, added to, or voided.

★ 4. What does it mean to you to know that God's promise is binding? What does it mean to you to know that your inheritance is secure?

★ 5. What are you free from? What are you free to?

DAY 4

Galatians 3:19–22

In proving his case for the truth of the gospel, Paul pointed out a number of times that God gave the promise before He gave the law. Knowing that the Galatians would likely all come to a similar question, he used one of his favorite teaching methods: asking—and then answering—that question for them.

Review 3:19.

1. What question about the law did Paul anticipate? Write it in your own words.

If you're interested in reading a *very* thorough answer, check out Romans 7–8. But in a nutshell, the law "was given alongside the promise to show people their sins" (Galatians 3:19 NLT). Held up against God's perfect law, the gravity of our transgressions is undeniable. The law shows us that we're sinners. And the law points us to our desperate need for a Savior. But more on that in a bit.

The law was given to God's people from God, by Moses, through angels (Deuteronomy 33:2; Acts 7:53). So Moses—or the angels, depending on which theologians you agree with[1]—served as the intermediary between God and His people.

★ 2. **Use a Greek lexicon to look up *intermediary*** (3:19). What did you learn?

Review 3:20.

When God gave His promise, He did so directly with Abraham, but when God gave His law, there needed to be a mediator. Later, when Jesus fulfilled the law, He *was* the mediator. God the Father, God the Son, and God the Spirit are one. The law required an intermediary between God and His people. But the promise included the intermediary Himself!

Anticipating another question, Paul offered some reassurance.

Review 3:21.

3. Complete the table below.

Question (in your own words):	
Reassurance (from each translation listed)	
ESV	*Certainly not!*
NIV, NLT, CSB	
KJV	

Even if the relationship between the law and the promise was difficult for the Galatians to understand—and even if that relationship is difficult for *us* to understand—this is certain: The law and the promise do not work against each other or cancel each other out. The law was needed, and God gave it. The promise was needed, and God gave it.

Review 3:22.

God's law, as recorded in Scripture, had a number of roles. Here, Paul taught that one of its roles was to reveal our sinful transgressions, "imprison[ing] everything under sin." We're all guilty. That's the bad news. But 3:22 doesn't stop there.

4. Complete the rest of 3:22 below.

   "But the Scripture imprisoned everything under sin, so that ____

   ________ ____ ________ in __________ __________ might be given

   to __________ _____ __________."

Like it did for first-century believers, the bad news helps us to cherish the good news. The law showed what was already true: With our sin, we built our own prisons and locked ourselves inside. And the same law pointed to the one who held the keys to our jail cells.

★ 5. Review the first question Paul asked today in 3:19. How would you answer it?

DAY 5

Galatians 3:23–29

"Before faith came" (3:23) means *before Jesus lived, died, and rose again*, which may seem contradictory considering Abraham's faith was just praised in the previous verses. In fact, many people from the Old Testament were praised in the New Testament for their genuine faith (Hebrews 11). But when Jesus came, faith was *fulfilled* and became sight. Martin Luther said it this way: "The faith of the fathers was directed at the Christ who was to come, while ours rests in the Christ who has come."[1] In other words, those who lived before Jesus came were saved by a forward-looking faith, and those of us who live after are saved by a backward-looking faith—a faith that is centered on the life, death, resurrection, and ascension of Jesus.

Review 3:23.

1. Based on what you learned on Day 4, what does "we were held captive under the law" mean? What did Jesus do for those who were imprisoned?

Review 3:24–25.

Explaining another role of the law, Paul used an analogy that would've been familiar to his audience. A guardian—*paidagōgos* in Greek—was similar to a private tutor or governess; they were common in wealthy homes of first-century Rome. A guardian, according to *Enduring Word*'s commentary, was entrusted not only with academic instruction, but also with moral education and discipline. When a child grew old enough, the guardian's services were no longer needed.[2] However, the instruction and guidance that the guardian had provided undoubtedly had a lifelong impact on the student.

The law is like that guardian, its instruction and guidance making a lifelong impact. The law instructed God's family in so many areas, and the law guided them to the good things that God loves, such as order, health, generosity, and worship. Jesus upheld and fulfilled the law, perfectly loving God and perfectly loving people. So while the law is no longer our guardian, its instruction and guidance still point us to God's heart.

2. Underline the part of 3:25 below that refers to the law. Circle the part that refers to Jesus.

> "Now that faith has come, we are no longer under a guardian."

★ 3. You underlined—but didn't cross out—the reference to the law above. Why is the lasting impact of the law important, even for Christians today?

Review 3:26–28.

Ancient Israel was designed by God to be a theocracy, meaning that He alone ruled. And since God's law was the law of the land, breaking the law, sinning, was a legal offense. In 3:26, the Greek word *huios*—meaning here "sons and daughters"—was a legal term. It was used in adoption proceedings and in covenants.[3]

So when God gave the law, it showed that sin had already made everyone criminally guilty. But believers can have confidence that God gave His Son and His Son made us legally innocent. What's more, His Son made us *family*.

Believing in Jesus and following Him makes strangers into family. So while every single person who has ever lived was created by God and bears His image, not everyone is God's child. In 3:26–27, Paul basically put it like this: *"Because of your faith in Jesus, you are God's children and His legal heirs. When your faith was decided, you became part of God's family. You put on new clothes!"*

So what does God's family look like? It's miraculously unified, and it's beautifully diverse. Distinctions among God's children exist, and Paul spoke to this reality in many places throughout his letters (we'll get to some of that in Ephesians). But the point of 3:26–28 is this: Old divisions, sinful prejudices, attitudes of supremacy, and actions of dominance have absolutely no place in God's family. Those are our old clothes. This verse doesn't advocate for uniformity. It invites us to unity.

★ 4. On the shirts below, write some words that describe our "old clothes," or our sinful ways before Jesus. Then, write some words that describe our "new clothes," or our lives shaped by Jesus. Some examples are listed for you.

Review 3:29.

Circling back and concluding his argument, Paul reminded the Galatians that the gospel was true and Jesus's work was complete. Understanding the law and its purposes was important for all Christ-followers—Jewish and Gentile. But *keeping* the law was not a requirement for salvation—it wasn't for the Galatians, and it isn't for us.

The legalism of the Judaizers wasn't just a problem then and there. It's a problem here and now. Many of us continually try to earn our place in God's family, even after we've already been adopted. And with our legalism, some of us try to convince our brothers and sisters that they have to earn their place too.

5. Write a prayer of repentance for the ways in which you've tried to earn your salvation or maintain God's approval of you. Or write a prayer of repentance for the ways in which you've tried to insist that others do the same.

Know this in your bones: If you are in Christ, you are Abraham's descendant. You are God's child. You are a dearly loved heir according to the promise God made thousands of years ago.

He created you. He adopted you. He gave you new clothes. He's making you more like Himself. And one day, He'll give you the full inheritance He promised long before you were born. And as one family, we'll praise Him forever, knowing He's where the joy is!

6. What stood out to you most in this week's study? Why?

7. What did you learn or relearn about God and His character this week?

DAY 6

Corresponding Psalm & Prayer

READ PSALM 19

1. What correlation do you see between Psalm 19 and this week's study?

2. What portions of this psalm stand out to you most?

3. Close by praying this prayer aloud:

Father,

The heavens declare Your glory! Your rules are true. Your commandment is pure. Your precepts are right. Your testimony is sure. Your law is perfect. And it's good to be in awe of You.

You've made me Your child and heir, but I've kept trying to put on my old clothes. You've declared me legally innocent, but I've clung to my own legalism. I've believed foolish lies about You, and my heart has wandered. Because You have declared me innocent from hidden faults, I freely and joyfully repent of my sins—intentional and unintentional—and I turn back to You.

Remind me every day of the truth and beauty of the gospel: It's by Your grace that I've been justified, and it's by Your grace that I'm being sanctified. Shape me to love the very good things You love—things such as order, health, generosity, and worship. Make me more like You.

Let the words of my mouth and the meditation of my heart be acceptable in your sight, God. I am Your servant. I surrender my life to You, Lord—every moment of my day, each decision I make, I yield my will and way to Your perfect will and way.

I love You too. Amen.

DAY 7

Rest, Catch Up, or Dig Deeper

WEEKLY CHALLENGE

In 3:19, Paul asked a short but weighty question: "Why then the law?" Understanding the roles of the law helps us, as Christians living thousands of years after God gave the law to the Israelites, grasp the big story of the Bible and our place in God's family. As theologians have reflected on the ways the law has served us, they've identified three specific uses of the law:

1. A mirror—the law shows us who we are: sinners in need of a Savior.
2. A curb—the law helps to maintain order and control violence.
3. A guide—the law points to the way we *should* live, which is the perfect way Jesus *did* live.[1]

In your journal or on a piece of paper, draw pictures representing each of the three uses as described above. Below each image, list examples of the ways you've seen this in your own life.

WEEK 4

Galatians 4

Scripture to Memorize

But I say, walk by the Spirit,
and you will not gratify
the desires of the flesh.

Galatians 5:16

DAILY BIBLE READING

Day 1: Galatians 4:1–7

Day 2: Galatians 4:8–11

Day 3: Galatians 4:12–20

Day 4: Galatians 4:21–27

Day 5: Galatians 4:28–31

Day 6: Psalm 105

Day 7: Catch-Up Day

Corresponds to Day 329 of *The Bible Recap.*

WEEKLY CHALLENGE

See page 103 for more information.

DAY 1

Galatians 4:1–7

Review 4:1–3.

Paul confirmed in 3:29 that the Galatians—regardless of what the false teachers were trying to get them to believe—were, in fact, already heirs. They were rightful sons and daughters of God through their faith in Christ, and he was going to prove it to them.

1. Fill in the chart using the word bank below.

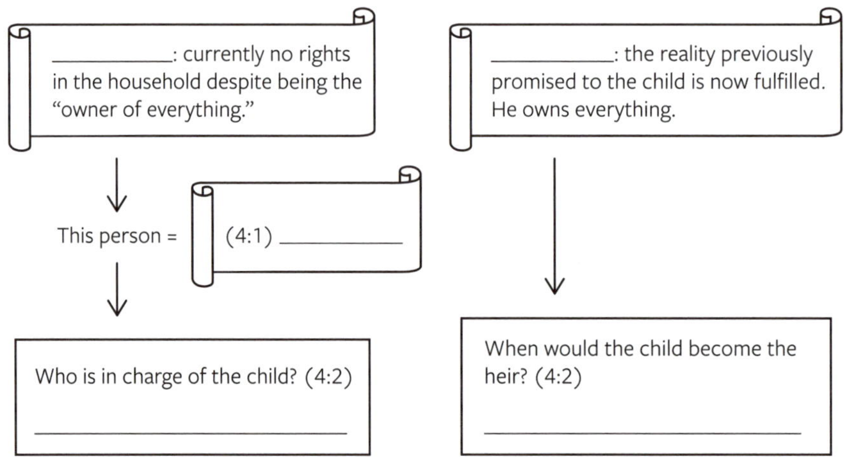

Word Bank

Adult/heir   Child/heir   Date appointed by father   Guardians and managers   Slave

Paul included himself as he related the metaphor of the child and slave to the Galatians. In their previous immaturity, both he and the Galatians had experienced slavery.

The phrase "elementary principles of the world" comes up twice in this week's reading, and scholars have different opinions about what it could mean. And to make things even more interesting, this phrase might have a different meaning in each instance. Let's unpack the two options for today's reading (we'll address the others when we get there tomorrow).

Option A: Paul might have been referring to the basic practices (or elements) of a religious belief system (Judaism or otherwise)—think rudimentary training, like learning your ABCs as the foundation of reading or how the periodic table of elements is the foundation of chemistry.

Option B: These principles (also translated *spirits*) might refer to demonic influence through the pagan practices of the Gentiles. Most believers in the Galatian churches would have previously worshiped idols—including the elements of nature like the sun, moon, and stars.

★ 2. Which option makes the most sense to you at this point in the study? Why? Use Scripture references where possible to explain your answer.

Review 4:4–5.

Thank goodness verse 3 isn't the end of the story (or paragraph). Just like Paul's analogy in which the father set a date for his son to receive his inheritance, God the Father also set a date for His Son—but the inheritance wasn't just for Him.

3. What two things describe Jesus in 4:4?

Paul emphasized the humanity of Jesus as a key piece of why He could be the one to redeem ("buy back") humanity. Because Jesus was fully man and followed the law perfectly, He was able to be the perfect sacrifice.

4. According to 4:5, what was the purpose of redemption?

A. Adoption
B. Legalism
C. Circumcision
D. Slavery
E. Freedom

According to Paul, the redemptive work of Jesus didn't *just* set humanity free from their slavery—the reality was even better than that. The redemptive work of Jesus invited people into the family of God to be adopted as God's kids.

Review 4:6–7.

Paul wanted to remind the Galatians that their status change from enslaved, immature, unredeemed people had already happened. They were already sons and daughters in God's eyes, and the proof came through the Holy Spirit. By the power of the Spirit at work in their hearts, the Galatians could rightly call God *their* Father.

All believers—Paul, the Galatians, and us today—are in the family of God through faith. And that means that all of us are heirs—not by our own works or attempts at righteousness, but through God.

5. Look back at 4:4–7 and fill in the actions you see from God (the Father), Jesus, and the Holy Spirit (the Spirit of His Son).

God the Father: ______________________________

Jesus: ______________________________

Holy Spirit: ______________________________

★ 6. What stood out to you in Paul's description of God's actions to bring about redemption? In what ways does this change or inform how you view God or yourself?

DAY 2

Galatians 4:8–11

READ GALATIANS 4:8–11

Many times in Paul's letters, he will seem to have finished his argument, only to circle back to explore the topic from another angle. He did that very thing here, and instead of emphasizing the change in the Galatians' *familial* status—from slaves to sons—he focused on their change in *spiritual* status.

Review 4:8–9a.

1. Fill in the table below with Paul's description of the Galatians' past and present realities.

Formerly: Pagan Gentiles	Now: Christians

Did you catch the relational emphasis Paul highlighted for the Galatians? Not only did they come to know God but they were now known *by* God. You might be thinking, *Wait, I thought God knew everything?* He does! But Paul's point here is not about God's omniscience. Instead, he wants them to see that God knew the Galatians even before they knew Him. Remember, He does the doing! It was God who initiated the relationship with the Galatians. This personal relationship with the true God stood in stark contrast to their previous relationship, which held them in bondage.

★ 2. Write down one or two ways God's relationship with you has brought you freedom.

Review 4:9b–11.

3. Circle the words that describe the "elementary principles of the world."

Weak Strong

Important Necessary

Worthless

Remember our two options from Day 1? (Take a look back if you need to refresh your memory.) Paul provided additional context here for how he might be using the term.

First, Paul referenced the Galatians becoming slaves *again* to these principles. He'd just gotten done reminding them of their slavery "to those that by nature are not gods." This reference to demonic influence supports option B.

Second, Paul highlighted the Galatians' current practice of observing "days and months and seasons and years." Interestingly, scholars think this could refer to either the pagan practice of astrology—seeking signs or wisdom from the stars—or their observance of the Jewish feasts and festivals.

Keep in mind that there's also a third possibility—perhaps Paul was using the phrase differently in each of these contexts. He might have meant astrology in 4:3 and Jewish holidays here in 4:9.

★ 4. Review your answer to Day 1's second prompt. Do you still agree with what you wrote? How do you think Paul used the term in 4:9? Use Scripture references to support your answers.

The main point Paul wanted the Galatians to understand was that they were free! Why in the world were they trying to enslave themselves to anything God didn't require of them?

The driving goal of Paul's life was to bring the good news to the Gentiles and welcome them into the family of God. He cared deeply for those he ministered to—including the Galatians. He worked hard, potentially to the point of exhaustion, so they could experience a relationship with God. And he hoped it wasn't in vain.

DAY 3

Galatians 4:12–20

We've seen Paul make some emotionally charged statements so far in this letter—he was astonished by the Galatians (1:6) and even called them foolish *twice* (3:1, 3). Here we see a few more emotionally charged statements and we get greater clarity on *why* Paul had every reason to be upset: The Galatians' behavior toward him had changed once the Judaizers came on to the scene.

Review 4:12–14.

As Paul painstakingly explained earlier in this letter, the Galatians were justified by faith alone. He also carefully reviewed the scriptural evidence for their freedom from the law. Their faith—by God's grace, *not* their works—changed their status from slaves to adopted sons in God's family. When Paul said, "Become as I am," he desperately wanted them to experience the freedom he had found in Christ.

1. In your own words, what does this passage reveal about Paul and the Galatians?

Paul:

Galatians:

2. How would you characterize the relationship between Paul and the Galatians when he first came to Galatia? Use Scripture to support your view.

No one knows for sure what Paul meant by his "bodily ailment," but it does seem to be the reason he was visiting the Galatians in the first place. Some scholars think he was sick with malaria and that the altitude in Galatia would have helped his recovery.[1] Others believe this referred to an issue with his eyesight—potentially a side effect of malaria or possibly a lasting result of the blindness he experienced when he encountered Jesus on the road to Damascus (Acts 9:1–19).

Review 4:15–16.

When they first met, the Galatians would've given Paul their very own eyeballs! (Perhaps this is another clue that Paul's bodily ailment referred to his eyes.) But not anymore! Paul had become their enemy and, worst of all, it was simply because he told them the truth.

★ 3. How do you react to godly correction from a friend, mentor, or pastor? How would you like to grow in this area?

Review 4:17.

4. Look up 4:17 in the NLT and NIV translations and fill them in below.

NLT:

NIV:

5. What seems to be the main motive of the false teachers? How does this differ from what you know about Paul's motives for ministry?

Zeal itself wasn't the problem. In fact, Paul pursued all God asked him to do with fervor (e.g., bringing the good news to the Gentiles). The problem was the Judaizers were zealous for lies, and their foolish passion was affecting the spiritual life and health of the Galatians. Zeal without knowledge leads to bondage (Proverbs 19:2; Romans 10:2–4), and the Galatians were falling prey.

★ 6. What are some ways you've seen or experienced the damaging effects of false teaching?

Review 4:18–20.

Paul desired goodness, freedom, and Spirit-empowered transformation for the Galatians. Using the metaphor of childbirth, Paul expressed his painful desperation for them to look more like Christ. Yes, he was their brother, but he also cared for them as a mother. He was devastated and confused to see his spiritual children be enslaved to the deceitful, self-serving false teachers. And like a good mother, he wanted to be *with* them again to offer explanation and clarity and draw them back to the only true gospel.

DAY 4

Galatians 4:21–27

READ GALATIANS 4:21–27

Review 4:21.

We don't know for certain whether the Judaizers were at church the day Paul's letter was read aloud. But if they were, this line might have been a direct shot at them. These false teachers, in their desire to be "under the law," submitted themselves and the Galatians to a form of legalism *never* required by God. This was Paul's repeated point: The gospel is good news and freedom, not legalism and bondage.

In submitting to the law, the Judaizers were actually forgetting the *whole law* as Paul understood the term. *Law* can mean the Mosaic law (the 613 specific laws given to Moses on Mount Sinai), and it can also mean the Pentateuch (the first five books of the Old Testament).

Paul planned to use the Judaizers' own methods against them. He would show them once more that the law was never about legalism, but instead had always promised and pointed to freedom.

Review 4:22–23.

1. Fill in the equation below.

   Abraham + __________ = son #1 (born according to the ______)

   Abraham + free woman = son #2 (born through _________)

Paul's point throughout this section is a simple one: Freedom is better than slavery. Let's briefly review the story he chose to illustrate his point.

The account of Abraham, Sarah, Hagar, and the two sons spans many chapters in Genesis (Genesis 12–21). Abraham's story started with a call and a promise from God: Abraham would one day be a great nation, he would have land, and the nations would be blessed through him (Genesis 12). As years passed and no child came, his wife, Sarah, offered a practical, human solution: Abraham could have a child through Hagar, her slave (Genesis 16). But as Paul pointed out, that child was born "according to the flesh." So where was the child of promise?

Despite Abraham and Sarah's taking matters into their own hands, God still fulfilled His promise by allowing Sarah to become pregnant at an old age. Her son, Isaac, was the true free child, born through the promise of God (Genesis 21).

Review 4:24–26.

Paul said this account could be interpreted allegorically. An allegory is "an extended metaphor in which the characters, places, and objects in a narrative carry figurative meaning."[1] Most allegories are works of fiction, but Paul knew that the narrative of Abraham, Sarah, Hagar, and their sons was true. He used their real story to create a relevant illustration in hopes of teaching the Galatians spiritual insights through a fresh lens.

2. Fill in the table below.

Covenant A: Slave Woman	Covenant B: Free Woman
Name:	Name:
Mountain:	Mountain: not mentioned
Present-Day Place:	Present-Day Place:
Status of Children:	Status of Children:

In Week 3, Day 3, we discussed covenants. God made many covenants with His people throughout Scripture. And the two covenants Paul mentioned were vital building blocks for how the Jewish people understood God, their history, and their destiny. Paul wasn't implying that one covenant was bad while the other was good. Rather, he wanted to emphasize that the basis for true relationship with God always came through believing God—both the promises He made and the truth of His character.

During the days of Jesus and Paul, many Jews held tightly to their heritage as children of Abraham (see John 8:33; Matthew 3:9). And the sign of the covenant for children of Abraham was circumcision. This was the Judaizers' claim—to become a child of God, you had to show you were a child of Abraham . . . *so get circumcised*.

The Judaizers could claim Abraham was their father all day long. But within this metaphor, Paul had a different question for them: Who was their mother?[2]

Review 4:27.

3. Write the commanded actions below.

Barren:

Not in labor:

★ 4. In your own words, why are they able to respond this way?

This reference from Isaiah promised bounty and fruitfulness to the people of Israel returning from a period of exile. During Paul's time, he saw this kind of abundance in God's family—a family full of Jews and Gentiles, freely worshiping God as children of promise.

★ 5. We covered a lot of ground today. What's one thing that was new to you or that stood out to you?

DAY 5

Galatians 4:28–31

READ GALATIANS 4:28–31

If you felt confused or overwhelmed at any point in Day 4, that's okay. Paul covered a lot of content from Genesis to make his point. Not only that, but he used symbolic interpretation (allegory).

Maybe some of the Galatians had questions, and perhaps that's why Paul explained to the Galatian churches where they fit into all of this. By the end of today's study, perhaps some of your questions will be answered too!

Review 4:28.

1. Use 4:28 and Day 4's second prompt to update the equation with the names of the people.

   Abraham + _______ = son #1, born according to the flesh

   Abraham + _______ = ______, born through promise

2. Who else did Paul call "children of promise"?

Review 4:29–30.

Paul was starting to draw the parallels between the Galatians and the people and events in his allegory. And he briefly alluded to one more story from Genesis about Abraham's two sons.

In Genesis 21, Abraham threw a party for his son Isaac—the son promised by God to Abraham and his wife, Sarah. The feast celebrated Isaac being weaned, so he was still young at the time—probably two or three. Abraham's other son—born from the slave woman Hagar, and probably a teenager at the time—laughed at (or mocked) Isaac during the party.

Sarah saw what happened and demanded that Abraham throw out Hagar and her son. Although Abraham was distraught, he sent Hagar and her son away.

3. Use 4:29, the word bank, and your knowledge of Genesis to fill in the blanks in the parenthesis.

"But just as at that time (__________) he who was born according to the flesh (____________________) persecuted he who was born according to the Spirit (_______), so also it is now (__________________________)."

Word bank: Isaac, son of the slave woman, Levi, Hagar, Sarah, Moses, Isaac's party, Judaizers persecuting the Galatians, Abraham, Jewish leaders persecuting Jesus

Paul certainly knew about persecution—he was beaten, run out of town, and thrown out of numerous synagogues as he faithfully preached the gospel. This persecution most often came from the Jewish leaders, Paul's own people, who claimed to be God's people—not because of their faith, but through their lineage with Abraham.

But Paul's point all along had been that the true sons of God came to know God through adoption into His family—not by simply being a son of Abraham. Because Abraham had *two* sons. And only one was born from a free woman.

4. Paul insinuated the Galatians should also cast someone out. Who?

The legalism the Judaizers preached to the Galatians was not good news. Their distorted, deceitful "gospel" led the Galatians directly into bondage. Why in the world would they choose slavery over freedom and lies over the truth? Paul was adamant the Galatians stop listening to the false teachers, and he went so far as to say they should throw them out.

Review 4:31.

Paul connected all the pieces as he closed out this lengthy metaphor. Abraham and the free woman had a son. This son was born through God's promise and Spirit. He was born free and destined for an inheritance.

The Galatians could also trace their lineage in God's family through a promise—God's promised Son. Jesus—"born of woman, born under the law" (4:4)—had redeemed the Galatians from idolatry and slavery. Through faith in God they were adopted into God's family. And the same is true for believers today. We are children of promise, adopted into God's family, and invited into freedom. Praise Christ! He's where the freedom is, and He's where the joy is!

★ 5. What stood out to you most in this week's study? Why?

★ 6. What did you learn or relearn about God and His character this week?

DAY 6

Corresponding Psalm & Prayer

READ PSALM 105

1. What correlation do you see between Psalm 105 and this week's study?

2. What portions of this psalm stand out to you most?

3. Close by praying this prayer aloud:

Father,

You made a covenant with Abraham, swore a promise to Isaac, and confirmed a statute to Jacob—and You remember it forever. You knew all of Your children long before we knew You, and it's good and fitting for us to praise You!

Like the Galatians, I've continued to enslave myself when Jesus has already made me free. I've tried to justify myself with my good works, when You alone are the one who justifies. And like the Galatians, I've made enemies out of Your servants and friends out of false teachers. I've pridefully rejected godly correction and sinfully embraced false teaching. I've chosen slavery over freedom and lies over the truth. Forgive me, God.

Help me keep Your statutes and observe Your laws—not so that You'll save me, but because You have already saved me. Remind me of the wondrous works You have done, Your judgments, and Your miracles. Let my heart seek You and rejoice always!

I surrender my life to You, Lord—every moment of my day, each decision I make, I yield my will and way to Your perfect will and way.

I love You too. Amen.

DAY 7

Rest, Catch Up, or Dig Deeper

WEEKLY CHALLENGE

Legalism has destructive consequences, which Paul highlighted throughout this letter. This week Paul reiterated the importance of the Galatians understanding they were free as sons of God. It's important to note that legalism is not the same thing as obedience.

Legalism (slavery) ignites the belief that we have to earn or maintain a right relationship with God through our own works. Obedience (freedom), on the other hand, is the Spirit-empowered way we walk out God's commands in response to His love for us.

Whether you've been a Christian for a long time or you're a new believer, it can be easy to fall into legalism. Are there any areas of striving in your life that don't align with the freedom you have as a child of God? This might look like ways you try to earn or keep your salvation, ways you seek to earn more favor with God, or even ways you fear He is punishing you for your sins and failures.

If so, write out a prayer of repentance in your journal. Ask God to remind you of the truth of your secure salvation, Christ's finished work on the cross, and the Spirit's indwelling presence in you as the sign and seal of your salvation.

WEEK 5

Galatians 5–6

Scripture to Memorize

For the desires of the flesh are against the Spirit, and the desires of the Spirit are against the flesh, for these are opposed to each other, to keep you from doing the things you want to do.

Galatians 5:17

DAILY BIBLE READING

Day 1: Galatians 5:1–6

Day 2: Galatians 5:7–15

Day 3: Galatians 5:16–26

Day 4: Galatians 6:1–10

Day 5: Galatians 6:11–18

Day 6: Psalm 15

Day 7: Catch-Up Day

Corresponds to Day 329 of *The Bible Recap*.

WEEKLY CHALLENGE

See page 128 for more information.

DAY 1

Galatians 5:1–6

READ GALATIANS 5:1–6

Review 5:1.

Throughout his epistles, Paul had a habit of making a statement and immediately following it with a command. This focus on putting the truth into action was likely due to his background in keeping the Mosaic law. Here, Paul summarized his message so far—*"Christ set believers free from the burden of keeping the law"*—and gave the Galatians a command: *"Stand firm. Don't return to law-keeping. It won't get you anywhere."*

The Jews couldn't justify themselves by keeping the law, so why did the Judaizers think anyone else could?

1. How did Paul illustrate their insistence on law-keeping? Fill in the blanks from 5:1.

"... do not submit __________ to a ________ of ____________."

A yoke is a wooden beam that connects two farm animals at the neck so they can pull a plow or cart together. The animals have to move in sync, because if one falls behind or pushes ahead, both feel intense discomfort and can't move forward. Eventually they can even end up going in circles, accomplishing nothing.

Through this illustration, Paul taught that the Galatians had been yoked to slavery—not literal slavery, but the burden of law-keeping. The law didn't save the Galatians or set them free; it enslaved them to a life of unnecessary striving—spinning in circles and gaining no ground.

Review 5:2–3.

Paul called for their attention—"Look"—and began to explain his command. And his explanation was simple: *Insistence on circumcision is a red flag.* Just as you can't call yourself a swimmer if you still have to hold on to the side of the pool, you can't hold on to the rules of the law and experience the freedom Jesus offers at the same time.

But what's the big deal? How would anyone know if you were circumcised? And why would anyone want to get circumcised?

Culturally, circumcision was a big deal because public nudity was normal, especially at public bath houses and athletic events. For Gentile converts, following Jesus meant rejecting pagan practices. This made them outcasts from the majority culture around them while also associating them with Jewish culture. That association may have been appealing, but the Judaizers were insisting that circumcision was *necessary* for salvation—and this wasn't just a bad idea or a poor choice. It was a complete distortion of the gospel; and a distorted gospel isn't the gospel at all—it's heresy.

The Judaizers wanted new converts to have faith in Jesus *and* keep part of the law—specifically laws about circumcision—but these two requirements were incompatible. It's like they were trying to mix oil and water. Additionally, Paul pushed the Galatians to think logically: You can't pick and choose from the law. If you keep one part, you're bound to all of it. So if circumcision was necessary, the Galatians needed to perfectly keep *all* of the law (which is impossible).

Review 5:4.

When sin entered the world, it created a problem: People were no longer in right standing before God. Because of sin, we all deserve death and are separated from Him. No one can solve their sin problem through their own works, performance, effort, or law-keeping. The only way to be saved is through faith in Christ.

2. Summarize the following verses in your own words.

Acts 10:38–39

Ephesians 3:8–9

1 John 5:11–13

★ 3. When you hear the phrase "a fall from grace," what comes to mind?

According to Paul, "fallen from grace" doesn't mean failing morally and losing salvation—we're saved by grace, not works (Titus 3:5; Ephesians 2:8–9). For Paul, falling from grace meant falling *into* legalism. Those two things—grace and legalism—are at odds. As one theologian said, "Grace is opposed to earning, not to effort."[1]

The Judaizers pushed this legalism, but Paul warned that relying on the law meant choosing to judge oneself by the law's standards instead of embracing grace. News flash: Nobody can meet those standards! We would all be doomed!

Review 5:5–6.

Righteousness isn't earned—it's given. The moment we're saved, God declares us righteous (our legal standing). But over time, as we continually surrender to the Spirit, we grow in righteousness and look more like Jesus (our transformation). This process is called *sanctification*. Paul longed for this, because he knew where it led. It leads to our *glorification*—when we'll be fully like Christ forever. And guess what? This future reality for believers doesn't have anything to do with circumcision.

So in the meantime, while they waited for glorification, Paul wanted the Galatians to remember that all Christian actions should come from faith and through love. Faith powers loving actions, because the believer is empowered by the Spirit after receiving salvation by faith (more on that later).

4. Draw a line matching the truths we learned in Week 1.

Gospel	faith→(leads to) salvation + works empowered by the Spirit
False Gospel	faith + works→(leads to) salvation

5. Circle the word or phrase that empowers all three of these things: faith, salvation, and works.

God's grace   Good luck   Hope   Self-discipline

DAY 2

Galatians 5:7–15

READ GALATIANS 5:7–15

On Day 1, we learned that salvation comes by faith, and the Spirit is given as a result of salvation. But what does that look like? This example is imperfect, but it might be helpful: Think of a lamp that isn't plugged in. It might look nice, but flipping the switch won't do a thing. However, once it's connected to a power source, it can shine like it was made to.

That's similar to one of the ways the Spirit works in us. Without Him, we're powerless. Paul knew this well. He relied on God's power at work within him. The Judaizers, however, depended on their own effort and persuasion—not God's power, love, and truth.

Review 5:7–9.

Paul compared the Christian life to a race (think of a marathon, not a sprint). The Galatians had started strong, but subtle distortions of truth had pulled them off track. According to Paul, any teaching about salvation that strays from Jesus's message isn't from God.

★ 1. What voices are you listening to? Think about all areas of your life (e.g., work, school, friendships, media, music, etc.).

2. Look back at our study of 5:2–3. Why are distortions of the gospel problematic?

Paul used a loaf of bread to illustrate this idea. Leaven is yeast, and it only takes a little yeast to make dough rise. Minor gospel distortions have major ramifications. While we aren't certain who Paul was talking about, it's clear that at a minimum, there was a single, leading voice spreading legalistic false teachings.

Review 5:10.

Instead of relying on his own effort, Paul relied on the Spirit's power. His confidence in the Galatians wasn't based on their ability, but on God's grace and faithfulness (Philippians 1:6; 2 Thessalonians 3:4–5). The power behind the true gospel supersedes that of all other teachings.

Paul was confident the Galatians wouldn't stay off track—not because they were strong, but because God is faithful and would hold on to them. At the same time, Paul made it clear that judgment was coming for the false teacher. He didn't say when, how, or even who "he" was, but he knew God saw (and sees) everything, and no one gets away with distorting the gospel. God keeps His people, but He also holds false teachers accountable for leading them astray.

Review 5:11.

Paul refuted the belief that he supported circumcision for Gentile believers. Some likely claimed this because he'd had Timothy circumcised (Acts 16:3). But that particular incident wasn't about salvation; it was about *evangelism*—it opened a door for Timothy to share the gospel with unbelieving Jews, who would've rejected him if he had been uncircumcised.

Paul willingly endured persecution for opposing the requirement of circumcision. He could have avoided that persecution by simply compromising. But he knew the gospel wasn't meant to be popular—it's offensive to many, because it shatters our self-reliance and declares that we can't save ourselves. Judaizers opposed him because his message undermined their works-based system and proclaimed total dependence on Christ.

★ 3. Have you ever engaged with someone who seemed to be offended by the gospel? If so, describe what that was like.

Review 5:12.

4. Look back at our study of 5:2–3. What were the Judaizers encouraging the Galatians to do?

Paul used provocative, exaggerated language to show how frustrated he was with the false teachers who were misleading the Galatians. While we shouldn't see his words as a model for how to treat others (after all, Jesus called us to love our enemies), there's something powerful here. Paul's passionate exclamation revealed his deep desire for people to know the true gospel. His outburst wasn't a command—it was an overflow of his heart. It's like Paul was saying, *"Let's stop this nonsense and get back to the truth!"*

5. Was there a time when someone in your life cared enough to point you back to the truth when you wandered off? Explain.

6. Have you ever had the opportunity to do that for someone else? Explain.

Review 5:13–15.

Christian freedom isn't about doing whatever we want; it's about loving and serving others in response to Christ and the Spirit. Paul reminded the Galatians that freedom in Christ isn't a license to sin; it's freedom from sin. But if they used their freedom selfishly, they'd end up serving the flesh instead of the Spirit.

That's why Paul affirmed, "*The entire law is fulfilled in one command: Love your neighbor as yourself*" (see also Leviticus 19:18). Without love, they wouldn't just struggle—they'd self-destruct. Turning on one another would tear them apart, but Spirit-led love would build them up.

DAY 3

Galatians 5:16–26

Review 5:16.

Yesterday's study ended with a warning from Paul: *Watch out! Don't self-destruct!* But in today's passage, he offered the Galatians a solution: *To avoid self-destruction, walk by the Spirit.*

Walking by the Spirit isn't a one-time decision—it's a daily, ongoing way of life. If the Galatians walked by the Spirit, Christ's victory would be at work within them. And that's not just a solution for them—it's God's design for all believers. Jesus called it *abiding*, and it's the only way for us to experience true joy and freedom in Him (John 15).

1. **Referencing a Greek lexicon, write the definition for the word *abide*** (John 15:4).

2. Read John 15:4–6. Fill in the blanks below.

"Abide in ____." (15:4)

"Whoever ________ in me and I in him, he it is that bears ________ ________."
(15:5)

"For apart from me you can do ____________." (15:5)

Review 5:17–18.

Though believers have been crucified with Christ, as long as we're on this side of eternity, our flesh and the Spirit will be in conflict (Romans 7:21–25).

3. What problem does Paul say the conflict between the flesh and the Spirit creates?

★ 4. Can you relate to this problem? Explain.

In 5:18, Paul dropped a quick reminder: The Galatians weren't under the law. Yes, the flesh can pull believers away from godly choices, but the flesh wasn't their only opponent—they were surrounded by outside voices. If the Galatians had answered the fourth prompt above, they might have drifted off track, likely mentioning a desire for circumcision. But Paul made it clear that their desires should be shaped by the Spirit, not the Judaizers.

Review 5:19–21.

The works of the flesh are outward signs of the battle between flesh and Spirit. So if signs of the flesh are frequently showing up in our lives, something's off. Walking in the flesh leads to sinful behavior, and sin left unchecked leads to death (James 1:15).

The patterns of our lives reveal what we truly believe. But it's important to note that Paul wasn't handing out a checklist of sins that disqualify people from heaven; after all, his chief message was that salvation is by faith alone. Many Galatians probably heard this list of sins and thought, *That sounds like me*. But Paul's point was deeper: Our choices reflect the state of our hearts. Paul was offering the Galatians a litmus test. If our lives don't align with what we claim to believe, it's a sign to pause and seek the Spirit's work in us.

Make no mistake—Christians *will* stumble. None of us will be perfect this side of eternity. But we shouldn't choose to stay stuck in sin. Repentance is a key sign of spiritual health. It's not too late to run from sin and sprint straight into the open arms of your heavenly Father.

★ 5. Circle the space on the continuum below that represents where you frequently find yourself. Why do you think that is?

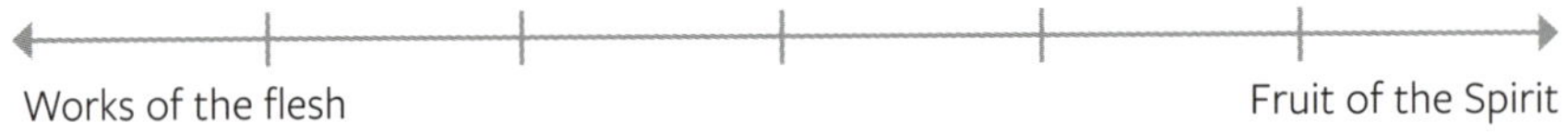

Works of the flesh — Fruit of the Spirit

Review 5:22–24.

Notice that "fruit" is singular. This is important. Paul wasn't listing separate traits but one unified result of the Spirit's work: Christlikeness. Think of an apple—it's not just red or green; it's also crisp, juicy, and sweet. In the same way, the fruit of the Spirit has many qualities—love, joy, peace, patience, kindness, goodness, faithfulness, gentleness, and self-control—but they all define one thing: *This* is what it looks like to be marked and empowered by God's Spirit. And His fruit grows more and more over time!

In contrast to the works of the flesh, fruit is evidence of a transformed heart—but *fruit takes time*. It isn't forced through effort, personality, or performance. It grows naturally when we surrender to the Spirit, which means it'll happen in God's timing, not ours. But if you're feeling discouraged, take heart. A farmer who plants an apple seed today won't wake up tomorrow to a full-grown tree. Fruit takes time, yet the Spirit is always at work.

6. What is sanctification? Look back at our study on 5:5–6 if you need help.

Crucifying the flesh is an active choice, but we don't do it alone. The Spirit empowers us. On this side of eternity, we'll never stop battling sin, but praise God, there's no condemnation for those who are in Christ (Romans 8:1).

Review 5:25–26.

Because believers have life in Christ and the Spirit's power, Paul urged the Galatians to make walking with the Spirit a daily habit.

All this talk about the Spirit and fruit may seem like a shift from the circumcision conversation, but it wasn't. Paul ended with a warning against arrogance and envy, the very attitudes the Judaizers were displaying. They insisted that their human striving and law-keeping was the best next step for the Galatians—but it wasn't.

DAY 4

Galatians 6:1–10

READ GALATIANS 6:1–10

Review 6:1–5.

1. According to 6:1, how were those who were spiritual supposed to restore the one who was caught in a transgression?

★ 2. If you knew you'd made a poor choice that other people in your church saw, how would you want them to confront you about it? What kind of conversation would encourage you to respond positively? What might tempt you to respond poorly?

The gist of Paul's instruction to the Galatians wasn't judgment or punishment. Instead, he taught that those who had fallen into sin should be corrected with the hope of restoration—and that's great news, because *all* believers are at risk of falling into sin (1 Corinthians 10:12). No one is exempt, because we live in a fallen world.

Burdens are also part of this reality—including sickness, financial stress, a natural disaster, or the consequences of our own poor choices. They're inevitable for us just as they were for the Galatians. So bearing others' burdens is *one way* believers can respond to these sad realities.

3. What is "the law of Christ"? Hint: Look up John 13:34–35 and write it below.

When we take our eyes off ourselves and consider others, we're much more likely to walk by the Spirit rather than yield to the flesh. The voices we listen to make a difference. When we aren't listening to the Spirit, we can be tempted to make much of ourselves. Paul encouraged the Galatians to find joy in their own sanctification and relationship with God instead of thinking they were spiritually superior to others.

4. Match each person with their respective description.

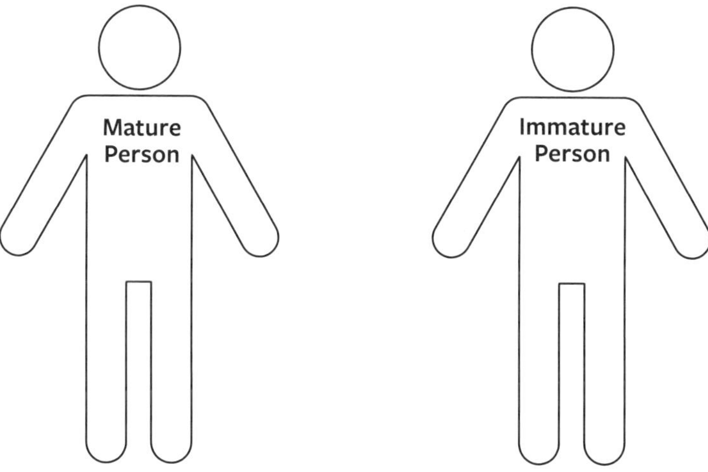

Recognizes their need to keep watch on themselves. They aren't immune to sin.	Is prideful, seeks division, and isn't self-aware. They aren't immune to sin.

In 6:2, Paul urged the Galatians to bear one another's burdens, but in 6:5, Paul said each person will have to bear their own load. So which is it, Paul? This isn't a contradiction. While Christians are called to bear one another's *burdens*, we're also accountable for our own *choices*. It seems Paul wanted to ensure the Galatians remembered that all people would have to stand before Christ's judgment at the end of their lives. Freedom in Christ isn't a free pass to sin.

Review 6:6.

Supporting spiritual teachers isn't about a financial transaction. It's about obedience. It's one way believers can love one another as Christ loved—selflessly caring for the faithful spiritual leaders in their community.

5. Review the illustration Paul used in 5:7–9. What did Paul want the Galatians to understand about the Judaizers' influence?

Galatian teachers may have been undermined by the influence of Judaizers. So Paul likely emphasized supporting faithful teachers to ensure the furtherance of the gospel. This financial support certainly wasn't about making the good teachers rich—it was about advocating for the proclamation of the one true gospel.

Review 6:7–8.

The Greek word for "mocked" here, *myktērizō*, means "turning up one's nose in disgust." But God won't let disrespect go without a response. Paul wanted the Galatians to grasp this, whether for themselves or the Judaizers.

Using the visual of planting crops on a farm ("sowing"), Paul contrasted two ways to live. Sowing to the flesh—indulging sinful desires—leads to destruction, while sowing to the Spirit cultivates holiness. The Galatians had a choice: One path led toward eternal life, the other to death. Paul made sure they felt the weight of it.

Review 6:9–10.

Just like a farmer waits for crops to grow, Paul urged the Galatians not to "grow weary of doing good." The rewards of "sow[ing] to the Spirit" would come—maybe soon, or maybe not this side of eternity—but they *would* come. In the meantime, patience and perseverance were key. God's timing for the harvest is always perfect.

★ 6. Describe a time when you were starting to "grow weary of doing good." Was there someone who encouraged you to lean on the Spirit and persevere? Explain.

Paul made a distinction: Believers should do good to all people, but especially to their faith family. Everyone bears God's image and has value, and we have a unique responsibility to care for our fellow believers.

This calling to care for others is rooted in Christ's example. Jesus lived a perfect life, carried our burdens, gave Himself for us, defeated death, and restored us to God. His life serves as the model *and* the empowerment for Christian service through His Spirit. But when we fail to follow His example, *He's still there.* His love never stops, and His mercy is new every morning (Lamentations 3:22–23).

DAY 5

Galatians 6:11–18

Review 6:11.

When it came to writing letters, Paul's practice was to dictate them to a scribe. But not here. Paul put quill to papyrus (or pen to paper), and his handwriting was distinct.

1. What was the distinctive feature of Paul's handwriting? Employ it when writing your answer.

While the size of his script may have been for emphasis, this personal touch also could have been a result of Paul's eyesight. Perhaps poor eyesight was the thorn in his flesh (2 Corinthians 12:7–9). Whatever the reason, Paul retained the main theme of his letter: Freedom in Christ is found through faith in Christ—not works.

Review 6:12–13.

The Judaizers wanted to make a "good showing in the flesh" by persuading Gentile Christians to get circumcised. On par with their striving and human effort, success was their goal. If the Galatians gave in (and pursued circumcision), their failure would've been the Judaizers' prize—making the Galatians the Judaizers' shiniest "trophy."[1] But faith in Jesus puts *His* work on display and doesn't leave room for pride or boasting.

2. Review our study of 5:11 (Day 2 of this week). Why might the Judaizers have insisted on circumcision?

Review 6:14–15.

The only thing Paul boasted about was the finished work of Jesus. Boasting in the cross means resting in Christ's finished work for salvation and then recognizing the role the Spirit plays—no personal efforts, achievements, or religious acts. Paul explained that alternative belief systems were "crucified to [him]," because they weren't a persuasive influence on him anymore.

External acts have never gotten anyone into heaven. The only way to become a "new creation" is through faith in Christ. This is what theologians refer to as *regeneration*.

Review 6:16.

Paul used the Greek word *kanōn* ("rule"), which referred to a measuring rod or standard. He likely compared belief in the true gospel to a rule because the *only way* to find peace, mercy, and freedom is through faith in Christ and the subsequent empowerment of the Spirit. There are no exceptions. If you're looking for salvation, don't work for Christ, *look to Christ*.

3. Compare Paul's words in 1:8–9 with his words in 6:16. Fill in the table below.

Anyone who preached a contradiction to the rule	
Anyone who walked by the rule	

When Paul used the phrase "Israel of God," he was referring to the rule keepers who'd received salvation through God's grace, by faith in Christ, unto God's glory. Paul took a familiar Jewish phrase, "the God of Israel," and flipped it upside down. It seemed he wanted to add some extra emphasis: *Jewish and Gentile believers alike are united in the family of God.* Entrance into God's faith family had always been based on faith—not law-keeping (Genesis 15:6; Romans 4:20–25).

Review 6:17–18.

Paul was resolved. The messages of people like the Judaizers didn't sway him. He knew what he believed, and he knew what it cost. Just as Jesus was persecuted, Paul had been wounded by those who rejected the gospel, and he had the scars to prove it. But make no mistake, Paul wasn't boasting in his battle scars. He was boasting in Christ—the one who continually empowered him by the Spirit to proclaim truth.

★ 4. Paul refused to live for the approval of man (1:10) and instead bore the physical marks of suffering for Christ (6:17). What evidence of faith—whether seen or unseen—might show in our lives if we truly lived for God's approval rather than people's?

Paul began this letter with grace (1:3) and ended it with grace (6:18). Grace is God's undeserved kindness freely given to us. Paul reminded the Galatians that they were brought into the faith family as his brothers and sisters *by grace alone*—not by works, not by rule-keeping, and not by circumcision, but by Jesus. What grace indeed! He's where the joy is!

5. What stood out to you most in this week's study? Why?

6. What did you learn or relearn about God and His character this week?

DAY 6

Corresponding Psalm & Prayer

1. What correlation do you see between Psalm 15 and this week's study?

2. What portions of this psalm stand out to you most?

3. Close by praying this prayer aloud:

Father,

You sent Your Son, who finished the work. Jesus, You lived a perfect life, carried my burdens, gave Yourself for me, defeated death, and restored me to our Father. If I boast in anything, may it be You! Spirit, You fill and empower me, and Your fruit in me is Your doing, and for Your glory.

I repent of submitting to the yoke of legalism and the burden of law-keeping. You've given me grace, but I keep scoring myself on my good works. I repent of abusing Your grace to serve the desires of my flesh. You've given me freedom, but I've used it as a license to keep sinning. Forgive me, Lord.

Spirit, as I walk by Your power, lead me to do what is right, to speak truth, to do no evil to my neighbor. As I walk by Your power, teach me to fear only You, God. Let me dwell on Your holy hill forever. As I wait for the glorification that will come with Your return, help me to abide in Your perfect grace. Come soon, Lord Jesus.

I surrender my life to You, Lord—every moment of my day, each decision I make, I yield my will and way to Your perfect will and way.

I love You too. Amen.

DAY 7

Rest, Catch Up, or Dig Deeper

Throughout our study of Galatians, Paul confronted the lie that says "faith + works = salvation." Unfortunately, this lie didn't stop in Galatia. In the sixteenth century, many saints of old followed in Paul's footsteps by standing for truth. Later, in the twentieth century, their defense of the gospel was formally summarized as the Five Solas (meaning "the Five Onlys").

Research the Five Solas. Create a bookmark for your Bible summarizing these truth-filled statements. Use Scripture references to support each truth.

INTRODUCTION TO EPHESIANS

After studying Galatians, Paul's letter to the church at Ephesus is a joyful shifting of gears. This letter is known as one of the Prison Epistles, which means Paul wrote it while he was imprisoned—this time in Rome in AD 62. You can read more about the circumstances of his imprisonment in Acts 28.

The church of Ephesus held a special place in Paul's heart. He pastored it for some time after Priscilla and Aquila founded it. The tone of this letter was one of a loving pastor discipling and mentoring his flock to maturity.

The first three chapters are primarily theological and doctrinal, which is to say that section highlights the foundation of what we believe. These are the essentials of the Christian faith. In the second half of the letter, Paul wrote about the practical application of those beliefs. This transition is fitting, because belief motivates behavior. In those three final chapters, Paul laid out expectations for the character and behavior of people who claim to follow Christ. He wanted them to be abundantly thankful for the hope and blessings of their life in Christ, and he wanted them to live in a way that reflected their heart transformation.

WEEK 6

Ephesians 1

Scripture to Memorize

Take up the whole armor of God, that you may be able to withstand in the evil day, and having done all, to stand firm.

Ephesians 6:13

DAILY BIBLE READING

Day 1: Ephesians 1:1–2

Day 2: Ephesians 1:3–6

Day 3: Ephesians 1:7–10

Day 4: Ephesians 1:11–14

Day 5: Ephesians 1:15 23

Day 6: Psalm 103

Day 7: Catch-Up Day

Corresponds to Day 350 of *The Bible Recap.*

WEEKLY CHALLENGE

See page 151 for more information.

DAY 1

Ephesians 1:1–2

1. Based on the introduction you just read, how is Paul's letter to the Ephesians different from his letter to the Galatians?

Review 1:1.

Paul's opening words to the Ephesians were filled with pastoral encouragement and theological depth. Unlike his letter to the Galatians—which addressed specific issues in their churches—this letter to the Ephesians broadly addressed Christian doctrine and its application. Despite these differences, you may have noticed similarities in his greetings to the two groups of believers.

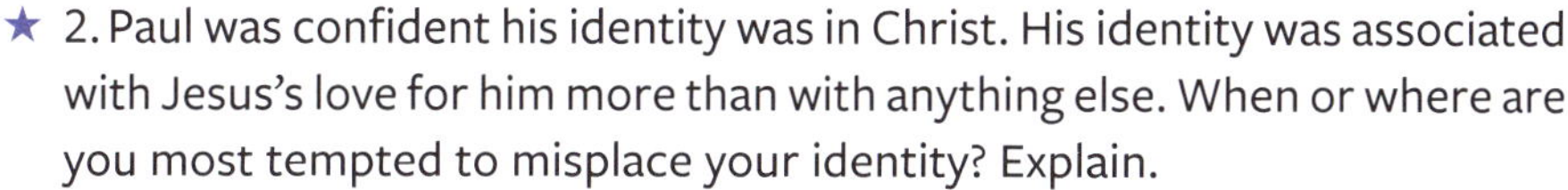

★ 2. Paul was confident his identity was in Christ. His identity was associated with Jesus's love for him more than with anything else. When or where are you most tempted to misplace your identity? Explain.

3. Go back to our discussion of the word *apostle* in Week 1, Day 1. In your own words, define *apostle*.

Paul knew the believers in Ephesus. He referred to them as "saints," which emphasized they were set apart for God. This nickname comes with a privilege: forgiveness of sins and adoption into God's family. But it also comes with a responsibility: living a life that reflects their set-apart identity.

4. How did Paul describe the Ephesians?

A. Hardworking

B. Faithful in Christ

C. Peaceful and gracious

D. None of the above

In this instance, the Greek word for "faithful" (*pistos*) has two possible meanings. It can refer solely to those who've received salvation through faith in Christ, and it can refer to people who are trustworthy *and* committed to living out their faith. In this instance, it's likely Paul implied both meanings.

5. Fill in the blanks in Ephesians 1:1 below.

"To the __________ who are in Ephesus, and are __________ in

_________ __________."

The Ephesians were "in" Christ. That means their identity and their position before God were defined by Christ. Theologians call this principle union with Christ. *Union with Christ* means that when we trust in Jesus, we're fully connected to Him—like a branch attached to a tree, drawing life from the source. Because of Him, we're forgiven, we're transformed, and we get to live in the never-ending joy of God's presence!

Review 1:2.

Most Greek letters opened with a traditional hello. But Paul went beyond this in his letters to both the Galatians and the Ephesians. The phrase "grace to you and peace" suggests a cause-and-effect relationship where grace leads to peace. (Hint: This has to do with salvation being by grace alone through faith alone.)

★ 6. The first two verses of this letter introduced us to some of its major themes. Based on what we know so far, fill in the table below. **(Use a Bible dictionary or Greek lexicon for help.)**

Theme	Union with Christ	Grace and peace	God's will
Definition		Grace: Peace:	God's perfect plan and purpose that always lead to His glory and our ultimate good.
Where does the theme appear in 1:1–2?	1:1—"faithful in Christ"		

DAY 2

Ephesians 1:3–6

READ EPHESIANS 1:3–6

1. In today's text, Paul used four versions of, or terms related to, the word *blessed*. **Using a Greek lexicon, match each "version" with its respective definition.**

1:3—"Blessed be the God"	*eulogētos*: praised
1:3—"who has blessed us"	*agapaō*: to be dearly loved
1:6—"he has blessed us"	*charitoō*: to give special honor, to make accepted
1:6—"in the Beloved	*eulogeō*: to cause to prosper, to make happy, to bestow blessings on

Review 1:3.

Paul recognized God's glory and goodness by using the phrase "blessed be." It expressed deep worship and adoration. He worshiped God in response to what he'd received from Him. God's blessings are guaranteed for believers, but know this for sure: Paul was writing about *spiritual* blessings, not temporary earthly "blessings." He wasn't praising God for things like money, good health, or success.

Review 1:4.

2. Fill in the blanks below.

"Even as he _________ us ____ him _________ the foundation of the world, that we should ____ holy and _______________ before him."

Paul was confident in God's eternal game plan—God chose to rescue people through Jesus. His mind had been made up since before time even existed! Make no mistake: Paul wasn't commenting on who would respond to Jesus in faith and who wouldn't. He was focused on what the plan meant for those in Ephesus who *had been* saved—who had been, to use Paul's words, "chosen."

Though we can't always understand how God works, Paul knew our response to God's mysterious work of saving grace should be praise. But why was he so confident? Just as we can be sure God has an eternal plan, we can be 100 percent certain all believers included in His plan receive spiritual blessings. In 1:4, Paul reminded the Ephesians of one of these blessings.

God chose to make us holy and blameless; theologians call this blessing *justification*. Justification is the beautiful truth that those who believe in Jesus are declared to *be* righteous before God. This isn't because of anything we've done. It's because of His grace and mercy. Justification describes our legal standing before God. Even though we don't always make holy choices and we're all deserving of death, our heavenly Father looks at believers—who have been saved by the finished work of Christ—and lovingly and permanently declares them not guilty!

Review 1:5–6.

3. Draw an arrow connecting the last two words of 1:4 with the first few words of 1:5.

"In love" "he predestined us for adoption"

Another spiritual blessing that comes with faith in Christ is adoption. In Roman law, adoption was irreversible, and it granted full familial rights to the adoptee. While a Roman could disown their biological children, they could never disown their adopted child. God's adoption of believers puts His love, kindness, and initiative on display. The parent initiates the adoption—not the child.

If the concept of God's will and believers being predestined for adoption makes you uncomfortable, take heart, and fight to cling to the character and goodness of God. His indescribable and incomparable love motivates Him to choose to rescue people through His Son and adopt them into His family. He didn't have to rescue anyone, but praise God that He loved us so much that He did—and is still rescuing people today.

4. Look back at our study of Ephesians 1:1–2. What is grace?

Just like justification was a blessing that moved Paul to praise, so was adoption. Paul praised God because he recognized adoption into the family of God was a result of God's grace, not human effort or striving. God's love for us is put on display through Christ. Moreover, Paul called Jesus "the Beloved." Scholars think Paul used this nickname for Jesus because it captured the Father's love for the Son. What God did in love moved Paul to respond in love, praising God for spiritual blessings that come with the gift of salvation.

★ 5. In your own words, summarize Paul's main point in 1:3–6.

DAY 3

Ephesians 1:7–10

READ EPHESIANS 1:7–10

Review 1:7a.

Paul continued writing about spiritual blessings, adding another blessing to the list: redemption. Redemption is something believers "have," which means it's a possession that can't be taken away. Just as the Ephesians were redeemed, believers today are redeemed as well.

1. Using a Greek lexicon, look up the word for "redemption" and write its definition.

Redemption indicates a price was paid, and the price for our freedom was Christ's blood. God paid our ransom by sacrificing His Son (John 3:16). Among other things, redemption brings freedom from sin's power *and* sin's penalty. Forgiveness means God isn't holding our sins against us—Jesus's death on the cross was the final (and only) payment. "It is finished" (John 19:30).

2. To help reinforce this truth, read Romans 3:23 and Romans 5:8, then summarize them below.

3. Paul was on a roll as he rattled off a list of spiritual blessings. Referencing Ephesians 1:3–7a, fill in the equation.

Salvation by grace alone, through faith alone, in Christ alone =

justification + adoption + ____________ + ____________ + ____________

Review 1:7b–8.

Redemption isn't solely our future hope. It is the present reality for believers—just as we were justified, so too we are redeemed. Through justification, we're declared righteous before God (our legal standing). And through redemption, the debt we owed God was paid (so we're forgiven and set free from sin). In Christ, believers experience complete forgiveness for all the sins we have committed, are committing, and will commit. This spiritual blessing isn't based on our works. It's based on God's grace, and it's our ongoing reality. What was true for the Ephesians is true for us today!

Paul seemed to be overwhelmed by his salvation and the goodness of God's redemption. He used descriptive words such as *riches* and *lavished* to describe God's actions toward believers. God doesn't have "just enough" grace or "just enough" forgiveness. His love and grace toward believers is immeasurable, and it isn't misplaced. He isn't careless or willy-nilly when it comes to His grace and the blessings that flow from it. He has a full understanding of every person at all times. He knows who He's committing to. And the God Paul wrote about chose to commit *to you*.

★ 4. How does it feel to be reminded that God redeems believers even though we don't deserve it? Describe a time when you were keenly aware of this reality in your own life. Does it produce gratitude and praise in you to recall this?

Review 1:9.

In the New Testament, a "mystery" often refers to a truth that's hidden from unbelievers but made clear to believers. The mystery of God's will isn't about day-to-day unknowns like "Where should I go to college?" or "Should I take that job offer?" This mystery is a greater, overarching truth: God's redemptive plan—which was only partially known to God's people in the Old Testament—is now fully revealed in Christ to those who believe in Him.

Those who don't believe in Jesus might ask, "How could anyone ever be in good standing before a holy God?" Now, believers know the mysterious question has an obvious answer: Through faith in Christ, we receive justification, adoption, and redemption. Our sins are forgiven!

Review 1:10.

Through Christ, God will and is unifying all things *in* Christ—both in heaven and on earth. His end goal is an ultimate resolution that's marked by the restoration of all that sin has corrupted. This future reality gives us hope!

5. Read 1:10 in the NLT. What phrase is used instead of "to unite all things in him"?

The Greek word for "bringing together" (*anakephalaioō*) calls to mind some simple math: addition—to add up, or to count until you arrive at a specified total. When Paul wrote about God's plan unfolding in the "fullness of time," he was reminding the Ephesians that God's plan is progressively unfolding in His perfect and trustworthy timing—not ours.

★ 6. Have you ever found yourself wanting God's plan to unfold more quickly? Explain.

DAY 4

Ephesians 1:11–14

Review 1:11.

God chose to rescue people through Jesus—and this plan had been in place since before time existed! By using the word *predestined*, Paul wasn't trying to explain who gets saved and who doesn't. He was unpacking the perks that those who *are* saved get to experience.

1. What have we received "in Him"?

   A. Cash
   B. Occupational success
   C. Favor with people
   D. A spiritual inheritance

This inheritance is certain—it's a guaranteed reality for those in Christ. Being included in God's family means benefiting from spiritual privileges and assurance.

2. Throughout our study of Ephesians 1, we've learned a lot about God's plan. Match each aspect of the plan with its definition. Use a Bible study tool if you need help.

If matching God's will to its definition was difficult, Romans 8:28 might help. God's plan doesn't exclude the bad or more challenging parts of our lives. When He says He works *all things* for His good purposes, He means it. Even if we sometimes struggle to understand what He's up to, we can trust that He is actively at work, using all things—the good, the bad, and the ugly—for His glory and our joy!

Review 1:12–14.

The fact that salvation is available to both Jews and Gentiles puts God's glory on display in a special way. The phrase "we who were the first to hope" referred to Jewish believers, as they were the first to respond to the gospel. So when Paul said, "you also," he was referring to Gentile believers in Ephesus.

Both Jewish and Gentile believers trust in Christ after hearing the message of salvation (a.k.a. the gospel). Salvation involves God's sovereign choice and initiative paired with our human response. The details of this arrangement can be mind-boggling—someday in the eternal kingdom, we'll have the opportunity to ask Jesus how this whole thing worked!

While we can't possibly understand all the details surrounding God's sovereign choices and the role our responses may play, we can praise God that there's something we *can* be certain about: our own salvation! As believers, we are sealed, and that's great news. Back in Paul's day, a seal was a "stamp that identified someone or authenticated something."[1] If something had been sealed, it was *verified*.

3. What alternative name does Paul give to the Holy Spirit in 1:14? Write it on the name tag below.

Paul described the Holy Spirit as a "down payment" or "guarantee"—*arrabōn*. This means that He is the first installment of what is to come (2 Corinthians 1:21–22). The Holy Spirit enables believers to live righteously while we await our future glorification.

★ 4. How does the presence of the Spirit offer assurance of salvation?

DAY 5

Ephesians 1:15–23

Review 1:15–16.

Paul offered thanksgiving after hearing of the Ephesians' faith and love. The faith and love they were marked by was evidence of the Spirit's work in them. Faithful and loving behaviors didn't *earn* them salvation—they *evidenced* salvation.

Through one lengthy sentence that began in 1:15, Paul elaborated on the contents of his prayers for the Ephesians.

1. How did Paul describe his prayers?

   A. Unceasing

   B. Incredibly lengthy

   C. Detestable

   D. Part of his daily Bible time routine

Review 1:17.

Paul prayed for the Ephesians to receive wisdom and revelation. He didn't ask God to give them supernatural abilities—he simply wanted them to know God more deeply. The phrase "the Spirit of wisdom and of revelation" seems to refer to either (a) the Holy Spirit imparting wisdom and revelation to the Ephesians or (b) the Ephesians' hearts being influenced by divine wisdom and understanding. Either way, more wisdom and revelation would've furthered their Christlike reputation or deepened their understanding of God's character and His plan.

2. Review our study of 1:9. What is the mystery?

Paul called on the "Father of glory," emphasizing God's majesty and power to reveal Himself. One key outcome of the Christian life is knowing God more deeply as false beliefs about Him fall away. Theologians call this spiritual illumination—God, through His Spirit, opens our hearts to more of His truth. Spiritual understanding doesn't come naturally or because of our own strength. He does the doing.

Review 1:18–21.

The "heart" represents the core of who we are; it's the place where knowledge and understanding live. When Paul mentioned the "eyes" of their hearts, he showed that the Ephesians' minds and hearts work together in responding to the Spirit and growing in the knowledge of God—and the same is true for us. Growth in Christ requires yielding to the Spirit.

3. Fill in the blanks in 1:18 below.

"... having the _______ of your _________ enlightened, that you may ______ what is the _______ to which he has _________ you, what are the riches of _____ glorious ________________ in the saints ..."

Circle the word *hope* in the third prompt above. In this instance, hope referred to both the spiritual blessings believers get to live in while on this earth *and* their future glorification.

Now put a box around the phrase "glorious inheritance in the saints." God values us as His treasured possession despite our imperfections—we fall short of His glorious standard. Nonetheless, He has invested love, wisdom, suffering, and glory in His people, making us rich in Him. Theologians interpret this phrase in two primary ways. It could refer to

a) God's inheritance in us (we are His possession)
b) Our inheritance from God (He gives spiritual blessings to us)

Either way, we're talking about something miraculous! Paul prayed that the believers in Ephesus would grasp the vastness of God's power at work in them.

★ 4. In 1:19, Paul described God's work. How do Paul's words help you better understand God's power?

The same greatness, power, and might that raised Christ from the dead empower believers to overcome temptation, doubt, and spiritual warfare (we'll study this more when we get to Ephesians 6).

After His resurrection, Christ was seated at the right hand of God. This confirms His reign over all things, as well as the honor and glory He shares with the Father, and it guarantees that believers will rule with Him.

Review 1:22–23.

Paul emphasized Jesus's supreme authority over creation. Christ's resurrection and exaltation led to God placing all things under His feet. God also included the church as one of the things under His feet—Christ is head of (the leader over) the body (the church). The church is the visible manifestation of Christ's presence in the world. This arrangement shows His authority over the *entire* universe.

In this particular passage, the phrase Paul used didn't indicate that Jesus is head of the church (though we do see that in one of Paul's other letters, in Colossians 1:18). Here, Paul showed us this truth from a different angle. He taught that Christ (in His appropriate role as head over all creation) is given to the church as a gift. What a gift indeed—to be led by Love Himself! He's where the joy is!

★ 5. What stood out to you most in this week's study? Why?

6. What did you learn or relearn about God and His character this week?

DAY 6

Corresponding Psalm & Prayer

1. What correlation do you see between Psalm 103 and this week's study?

2. What portions of this psalm stand out to you most?

3. Close by praying this prayer aloud:

Father,

With everything that is within me, I bless Your holy name! You're merciful and gracious, slow to anger, and abounding in steadfast love. You forgive my iniquity, You heal my diseases, You redeem my life from the pit.

You've made me a saint—set apart for You. I've embraced the privilege of my sainthood—Your forgiveness of my sins. But I've neglected my responsibility; I haven't lived a life that reflects my set-apart identity as Your child. Forgive me.

Remind me that Your steadfast love for me is as high as the heavens above. May Your love and work in me lead to holy and righteous living.

As I wait for the fullness of time, I surrender my life to You, Lord—every moment of my day, each decision I make, I yield my will and way to Your perfect will and way.

I love You too. Amen.

DAY 7

Rest, Catch Up, or Dig Deeper

WEEKLY CHALLENGE

In Ephesians 1, Paul mentioned each person of the Trinity (Father, Son, and Spirit). While the word *Trinity* is never used in Scripture, the doctrine is woven throughout the Word. Ephesians 1 is one of many passages that helps our understanding of the Godhead.

Do some research. How is each person of the Trinity presented in Ephesians 1? How does your understanding of the Trinity impact your understanding of this week's passage?

WEEK 7

Ephesians 2–3

Scripture to Memorize

Stand therefore, having fastened on the belt of truth, and having put on the breast-plate of righteousness . . .

Ephesians 6:14

DAILY BIBLE READING

Day 1: Ephesians 2:1–10
Day 2: Ephesians 2:11–22
Day 3: Ephesians 3:1–6
Day 4: Ephesians 3:7–13
Day 5: Ephesians 3:14–21
Day 6: Psalm 95
Day 7: Catch-Up Day

Corresponds to Day 350 of *The Bible Recap*.

WEEKLY CHALLENGE

See page 177 for more information.

DAY 1

Ephesians 2:1–10

READ EPHESIANS 2:1–10

In this section of Ephesians, Paul painted a picture of the past, present, and future of every believer. While it begins with a dismal reminder of the dark path behind us, it quickly points to our ultimate purpose, which is initiated, sustained, and fulfilled by God Himself!

Review 2:1–3.

1. List the ways every believer once walked when they were apart from Christ.

Paul pulled no punches in describing the Ephesians' spiritual state before they were saved by Christ. To be "dead" in our trespasses and sins means we are completely separated from God. As Paul could attest, living apart from God is no life at all.

Paul will expound on this "power of the air" near the end of the letter, but here, his point was to remind the Ephesians where they came from. He didn't do this to condemn them. In fact, this laid the groundwork for a great celebration of what Jesus had done for them—but not *just* for them.

2. Who did Paul include as he recounted their former lives of trespasses and sins?

A. Gentiles
B. Jews
C. Everyone but himself
D. All of humankind

Let this truth kill the comparison game the enemy likes to plant in our minds. Even "Pastor Paul" identified himself as someone who carried out the desires and passions of his flesh—someone who, by his very nature, was a *child of wrath*. The culture then wasn't so different from ours now. Certain preachers and orators were elevated based on their skills, charisma, and knowledge. It's all too easy to place these people on a pedestal and compare ourselves to them, convincing ourselves that our past is too dark for us to be used by God. Lies like these are one reason why reading God's Word is so good for our souls—He tells a much different story than the flesh and the enemy, and it's one of grace and redemption.

Review 2:4–7.

While Paul reminds us of our past, he doesn't leave us there. In fact, it's as if he puts a hand under our chin, gently lifts our head, and looks us dead in the eye to say: "*But God . . .*"

3. What was God's motive for rescuing us?

Notice who "does the doing" in this passage. We were dead men. Christ did for us what we could not do for ourselves.

4. Match the action God took with the one who empowers us.

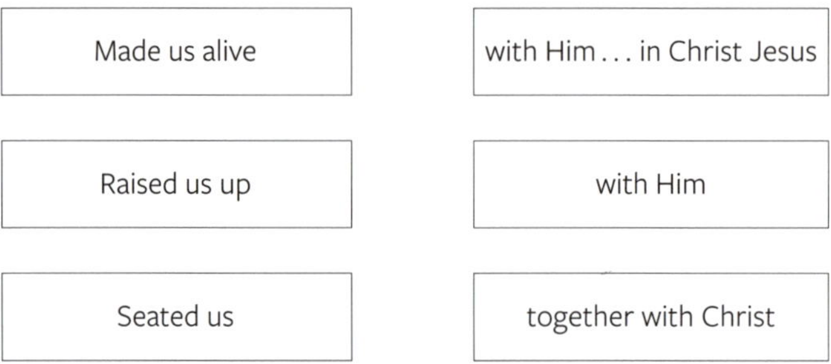

Reread 2:6, then look back at 1:20–22.

This is more than just a shift in our eternal destination—it's a shift in our status and authority *now*. The Ephesians were a faithful, growing, committed body of believers—something the prince of darkness and the "sons of disobedience" hated. Paul knew the church would come under physical and spiritual resistance to the work God was doing in them. But the prince of the power of the air is no match for the Creator of the universe, and Paul wanted them to remember that they carried His authority now—and so do we. This is merely a taste of the "immeasurable greatness of his power" (1:19) and the "immeasurable riches" (2:7) available to us through His grace.

Speaking of grace . . .

Review 2:8–9.

Don't let the familiarity you may have with this passage cause you to detach from the powerful reminder these verses carry. Camp out here for a moment.

★ 5. What two gifts did Christ supply to bring about your salvation? Do you believe these truths? Have you fully let go of the responsibility of saving yourself?

6. On the scale below, circle the number that represents how much pride you take in establishing your own salvation. Then, draw a square around the number that represents how much you *should* boast.

Review 2:10.

★ 7. Read Philippians 2:13. In light of this verse and today's passage, who is the one supplying you with the power to do good works? Have you experienced this? If so, describe your experience.

When we can let go of the stress, angst, worry, and impostor syndrome that come from trying to muster our own power, Christ does work through us that is—as Paul likes to say—*immeasurable*.

DAY 2

Ephesians 2:11–22

READ EPHESIANS 2:11–22

Paul began this hearty section with an important *therefore*. This word was intentionally placed as a reminder of the good news he had just shared with them: the gifts of grace and faith. This *therefore* set his audience up for even more good news: These gifts are for all humankind.

Review 2:11–12.

Paul turned his attention directly to the Gentiles (referred to here as "the uncircumcision") to remind them why their spiritual state had been so dire. But he also had a message for the Jews ("the circumcision").

It's true that physical circumcision was the sign of God's promise to Israel (Genesis 17), but as we'll see in the coming verses, it was never God's plan to exclude other nations from His grace.

1. In the Before column, list the description Paul gave of the Gentiles' spiritual state in 2:11–12, before the gospel came to them. We'll come back to the After column later. The last two answers in each column have been provided for you.

Before	After
Hopeless	Reconciled to God
Without God	Members of God's household

★ 2. How would you describe your own spiritual state before the gospel came to you?

Review 2:13–17.

Before Christ commissioned the apostles to go to all nations (Matthew 28:19), the future for the Gentiles was bleak, to put it mildly. As Paul said, they had no hope in the world. But in 2:13, you can almost picture Paul, who is "of the circumcision," raising his finger as he made a crucial point on behalf of "the uncircumcision." He said, "But now in Christ Jesus . . ." And with that phrase, Gentiles everywhere could take a collective breath.

★ 3. In the context of this passage, what do you think it means for Christ to "be our peace"—not just to provide peace, but to actually be our peace?

We know from our introduction that Paul was in prison when he wrote this letter. The reason for his imprisonment was that he was accused of allowing a Gentile to come past the wall that divided Jews and Gentiles at the temple (Acts 21:27–29). So when Paul said that Christ breaks down the dividing wall of hostility (see 2:14, 2:16), he was speaking both literally and spiritually—and for him it was personal.

4. Go back to the table in today's first prompt and fill in the After column with all the ways God reversed the curse for Gentile believers.

Review 2:18–22.

If you write in your Bible, circle or highlight where you see the three persons of the Trinity in 2:18. Because of Christ's sacrifice and the Spirit's power, we have access to the very throne room of God (the Father).

In 2:20, Paul used the illustration of Christ Jesus as the cornerstone. This isn't a simple preaching metaphor to help him tell a story. The idea of Christ as the cornerstone appears throughout the Old and New Testaments, in the writings of the prophets and the apostles.

In ancient architecture, the cornerstone was the most vital component of the entire project. It provided both stability and alignment as the rest of the structure came together. While the different elements of the structure were separate and provided support for the building as a whole, the cornerstone held them together correctly—distinct, but unified.

5. **Using a Bible study tool, find as many references as you can to the cornerstone in both the Old and New Testaments and write them in the empty bricks below.** The first one is provided for you.

Paul's point in this section was the unity that is available between Jew and Gentile as they are reconciled to God. Speaking directly to the Gentiles, and putting on his proverbial hard hat, he sketched out a beautiful blueprint that included them as "fellow citizens . . . members of the household . . . joined together . . . built together"—and all of this was so that they could, together, be a dwelling place for God by the Spirit.

6. God is the pathway by which all this unity is possible. From today's passage, fill in every mention of persons of the Trinity as the conduit of unity. Some answers are provided.

2:13 ____

2:14 He Himself, in His flesh

2:15 ____

2:16 ____

2:17 ____

2:18 through Him, in one Spirit

2:19 ____

2:20 ____

2:21 ____

2:22 in Him, for God, by the Spirit

Now, in 2:22, imagine that Paul turns his attention to you. "In him you also . . ." No matter who you are—no matter your race, ethnicity, gender, or location—if you are in Christ, you also are being joined with other believers as a dwelling place for God. What grace!

DAY 3

Ephesians 3:1–6

Previously in our study, Paul mentioned a "mystery" that had been revealed to him—that one day Christ would unite all things in Him (1:9–10). Here, we see Paul getting more specific: The mystery had deeper implications that explained his current state of affairs.

Review 3:1–3.

We begin with the words "For this reason," which call us back to the previous section about the unity of the church. But the church was incomplete without the Gentiles. "For this reason" Paul was a prisoner on their behalf.

1. According to 3:1, who was Paul a prisoner of?

   A. The Romans

   B. Christ

   C. The Gentiles

   D. The Jews

Paul may have been under Roman lock and key, but he knew that nothing happened outside of God's plans, and he was God's "chosen instrument" to take the gospel to the Gentiles (Acts 9:15). So as long as he was living, he was a servant of Christ for this purpose.

★ 2. How are you encouraged by Paul's resolve despite his circumstances?

Review 3:4–5.

Paul likely had his readers and listeners on the edge of their seats as they waited with anticipation for this revelation that even "the sons of men in other generations" had been blinded to.

Review 3:6.

3. The mystery was threefold. Paul revealed that the Gentiles are . . .

A. ____________________

B. ____________________

C. ____________________

Imagine you're watching a detective show, and little pieces of information have been sprinkled throughout the episode. You've seen the different puzzle pieces, but you're not sure how they fit together until the moment of the big reveal. And suddenly, lightbulbs start going off in your mind—flashbacks to pieces of the puzzle, clues along the way—and you realize the truth was right there all along, hidden in plain sight.

4. Fill in the table with clues found throughout the Bible to God's plan for the Gentiles.

Verse	What Was Revealed
Psalm 86:9	
Zephaniah 3:9	
Isaiah 66:23	
Psalm 117:1	

What does this tell you about God's plan all along?

For Jews and Gentiles alike, God had hidden this mystery in plain sight throughout the Old Testament. In the New Testament, it all culminated in a violent moment between a confused mob and a carpenter in Nazareth.

In Luke 4:14–30, Jesus revealed Himself as the long-awaited Messiah to the Jews in the synagogue. At first, the crowd was overjoyed at Jesus's proclamation. In fact, Luke said they "were amazed at the gracious words that came from his lips" (Luke 4:22 NIV). That is, until Jesus pointed out that His grace extended to people of other nations—people who had been their enemies. For His Jewish listeners, this was a bridge too far, and they tried to kill Him. Can you imagine going from praise to attempted murder in a matter of moments? This is how divisive and offensive God's great love can be when it infringes on our personal values.

★ 5. Why do you think the Jews had so much trouble accepting this sort of unity with Gentiles? Where do you sometimes see a struggle for unity in the body of Christ?

This was the very issue Paul had been commissioned by God to address. He wrote about this in Romans, we saw it in Galatians, and here we are again—this is the great mystery revealed.

Paul, also a Jew, understood the shock of his fellow countrymen. Despite having been incredibly familiar with God's Word, including the passages from today's fourth prompt, they seem to have been caught off guard by God's lavish generosity to the people of all nations. As we saw in those Old Testament passages, God has always been promising that salvation would come *through* Israel *to* the world—and that promise was fulfilled in Jesus. His one unified body—made up of Jews and Gentiles alike—became known as the church.

The apostle Peter was also shocked when God revealed this mystery to him in Acts 10–11.

6. Fill in the blanks in Acts 11:17.

"If then God gave the same gift to [the Gentiles] as he gave to us when we believed in the Lord Jesus Christ, ______ ______ ___ ________ ___ ___________ _________ ___ _________ ______?"

Paul had, at one time, stood in God's way. But no more. He'd found his purpose, and "for this reason" he was willing to be in chains.

DAY 4

Ephesians 3:7–13

READ EPHESIANS 3:7–13

Review 3:7–9.

On Day 2, we learned that the Gentiles had been separated from God and without hope. So what might it have meant to them to know God had a plan for them all along? Paul could affectionately empathize with the wonder they might've felt, knowing that he, too, was simply a product of God's grace.

1. What word did Paul use to describe grace? (Hint: He used the same word in 2:8.)

2. According to 3:8, how did Paul see himself compared with the other saints?

Paul knew he was in no way better than anyone else. The gift the Ephesians needed for salvation was the same one afforded to him that he might preach the gospel. Before Christ, Paul spent his life aspiring to be a religious leader among the Jews. Now, as a minister to the Gentiles, he was happy to be made low as a servant of Christ. He spoke of "unsearchable riches" knowing he was no longer living for glory, prestige, power, or material prosperity. Christ's unsearchable riches meant something much greater—living in the immeasurable peace of God's grace.

★ 3. It's clear that Paul didn't feel he *had* to serve Christ but rather that he was blessed to serve Him. Describe the difference. Why do you think he found so much joy in preaching to the Gentiles?

Review 3:10–11.

Ponder 3:10 and marvel. It's exactly what it sounds like. God's plan, since the creation of the world, has been to use the church to reveal His manifold (many-faceted) wisdom to angelic beings. This verse reveals an incredible truth: The rulers and authorities in the heavenly places will know God better because of His work *in us*.

It's worth noting that these rulers and authorities refer to angelic beings that are both good and evil (if this surprises you, check out 1 Timothy 5:21 and 2 Peter 2:4). As God moves in the hearts of His people, the angels will look on in wonder, and demons will observe and shudder. This has been God's plan all along, and it was accomplished through the work of Jesus.

Review 3:12.

★ 4. Next to each of the phrases below, write what they mean to you in your personal relationship with Christ:

We have boldness:

Access with confidence:

Faith:

Boldness here is translated from the Greek *parrēsia* and carries the idea of "freedom of speech." In other words, because of Christ, you can speak freely before God. In fact, Psalm 116:2 says God inclines His ear to listen to our prayers. When you talk to Him about *anything*, imagine Him leaning forward in love, eager to hear everything you have to say—the good, the bad, and the ugly.

5. Is this how you envision God when you pray? Why or why not? Is there anything you think you can't talk to God about? Why?

Review 3:13.

6. Why might the Ephesians have been in danger of losing heart? Has there been a time in the past when you felt like you were losing heart? How did God strengthen your heart during that time?

Paul had suffered many things in the name of taking the gospel to the nations. He described his trials in 2 Corinthians 11:24–28. It's quite the list of physical, mental, spiritual, and emotional affliction. And here, he was suffering again. *Why* would someone endure so much pain?

7. What was Paul's explanation in 3:13? How might this have encouraged and emboldened the Ephesian churches?

Paul could not have endured all of this without the power of God inside him. A person can only take so much. But God had poured out His Spirit on Paul and sent him out—and He has done the same for us. As we move into the second half of Ephesians, you'll hear more about what it means to live as a servant of Christ. And there may be times when you wonder if you're up for the challenge. Let Paul serve as an example *you're not*. But the Spirit living inside you will empower you. He does the doing.

DAY 5

Ephesians 3:14–21

READ EPHESIANS 3:14–21

You've reached the halfway point in the book of Ephesians! In Ephesians 1–3, Paul encouraged his audience with the truth of the gospel and the unity of God's family. In Ephesians 4–6, Paul will call on followers of Christ to live in a way that reflects the overflow of God's grace. Nestled between these two halves is a prayer for all believers. Settle in and let Paul's prayer wash over you and remind you of God's power and His loving-kindness toward you.

1. Paul prays a four-part intercessory prayer for each of the believers. Before we examine each part, can you identify his four requests?

Verse	Request
3:16	
3:17a	
3:17b–19a	
3:19b	

Review 3:14–16.

Calling their attention to God's power and sovereignty from the very beginning of his prayer, Paul reminded the Ephesians that God is the head over all creation, "every family in heaven and on earth." It's from His power that we get our strength.

2. What do you think it means to be strengthened in your inner being? Have you felt this during a time when you didn't feel especially strengthened in your *physical* being?

Review 3:17–18.

This concept of Christ dwelling in our hearts is the same idea we see in the Old Testament of God's presence dwelling in the temple (2 Chronicles 7:1–3). We know from 1 Corinthians 6:19 that our bodies are a temple for the Holy Spirit, and here in Ephesians 3:17, according to Enduring Word's commentary, the word *dwell* conveys the idea of Christ taking up *permanent* residence in our hearts.[1]

★ 3. What do you think it means to be rooted and grounded in love?

If you want to operate in the confidence and power of Christ, you have to get this truth deep into your bones: You are deeply, unconditionally, wholeheartedly, eternally loved by Jesus. His love is so vast that it's immeasurable.

Review 3:19.

When Paul was a student of the law, he was filled with knowledge about God. As a Pharisee, he probably had the first five books of the Bible *memorized*. Let that sink in. But simply having knowledge never fulfilled the needs of his heart. Only a Savior could do that. Paul knew from experience that the Ephesians would need to know love that *surpasses* knowledge. They would need to know Christ's love by experiencing it for themselves.

4. Was there a time when you knew Christ's love by experience—when the dots connected between your head and your heart, and you knew you were being cared for by God? If so, briefly describe. If not, write out (and pray) the part of Paul's prayer recorded in 3:19.

Paul's final request was that the Ephesians might be "filled with all the fullness of God"—that they would continue growing and maturing in their faith.

Review 3:20.

Paul laid his requests before God on behalf of the Ephesians, then he essentially ended his prayer with *"or do something better."*

As we're fervently praying, we think we know what we need. But as we cry out to a sovereign God who loves us more deeply than we can comprehend, we do well to make requests of Him and then leave the results in His hands. If He doesn't answer the way we think He should, we can trust that He is doing something better—something far more abundant than all we ask or think.

5. What is burdening your heart? What are you crying out to God for? Instead of making the request again, write out a prayer thanking Him that He is able to do abundantly beyond all you can ask or even *think* to ask.

Review 3:21.

We saw on Day 4 that God is going to do a unique work through the church to make His wisdom and power known in heaven and on earth. How is this possible? Because He is dwelling in the hearts of every believer, He makes His presence known through *you*. And because of *His* power at work in your life, people of all generations will know by experience that beyond all doubt, He's where the joy is!

★ 6. What stood out to you most in this week's study? Why?

7. What did you learn or relearn about God and His character this week?

DAY 6

Corresponding Psalm & Prayer

READ PSALM 95

1. What correlation do you see between Psalm 95 and this week's study?

2. What portions of this psalm stand out to you most?

3. Close by praying this prayer aloud:

Father,

You are a great king, and a great God—the God above all gods. You hold in Your hand the depths of the earth and the heights of the mountains. You made the sea and the dry land. And You made me in Your very image. I was dead in my sins, but You rescued me and adopted me into Your family! You created and redeemed me. Like the psalmist, let that truth lead me to worship and bow down. Like Paul, let that truth lead me to kneel before You, my maker and my Father!

You made me Yours, but at times, I've turned my heart from You and gone astray. I've tried to place myself as a cornerstone, making much of myself and little of You. Or I've refused to believe that Your saving grace is sufficient, again making much of myself and little of You. I repent.

May the truth of Your glory leave me in awe. May the goodness of Your presence lead me to rest in You. May the beauty of how much You love me live deep in my bones. As I bring all of my longings to You, may I hold them with open hands, praying, "Or do something better, God"—like only You can.

I surrender my life to You, Lord—every moment of my day, each decision I make, I yield my will and way to Your perfect will and way.

I love You too. Amen.

DAY 7

Rest, Catch Up, or Dig Deeper

WEEKLY CHALLENGE

On Day 1, we learned about the state of our hearts before we met Christ—how dark and hopeless we were, following the "course of this world" (2:2). But Paul shared a phrase that is the turning point of grace in every believer's life: "But God . . ." (2:4). Paul wrote out a testimony that applies to all of us, the testimony of the finished work of Christ.

Using pen and paper or other art tools, write the phrase *BUT GOD* at the top of the page. Below that heading, write each of the things you see God doing in 2:4–10. Then pray for an opportunity to share the things you just wrote (the testimony of Jesus) with someone who wouldn't consider themself a Christian.

WEEK 8

Ephesians 4

Scripture to Memorize

. . . and, as shoes for your feet, having put on the readiness given by the gospel of peace.

Ephesians 6:15

DAILY BIBLE READING

Day 1: Ephesians 4:1–6
Day 2: Ephesians 4:7–16
Day 3: Ephesians 4:17–24
Day 4: Ephesians 4:25–29
Day 5: Ephesians 4:30–32
Day 6: Psalm 68
Day 7: Catch-Up Day

Corresponds to Day 350 of *The Bible Recap*.

WEEKLY CHALLENGE

See page 200 for more information.

DAY 1

Ephesians 4:1–6

READ EPHESIANS 4:1–6

Review 4:1.

As you read in the introduction, Ephesians 1–3 focused on the theological truths Paul wanted to express to his beloved Ephesians. As he waited under house arrest in Rome, he wrote to his friends about the majesty and glory of their God—His kindness in redemption, His lavish love, and His glorious plan for Jews and Gentiles to be unified in one family.

By using the word *therefore* in 4:1, Paul reminded the Ephesians that everything he'd just written—and all that you've studied these past weeks—is connected to the rest of the letter. The Ephesians were called to consider how to apply these truths in their lives, relationships, and church, and the same is true for us today.

Here, Paul called the Ephesians to *walk*. The calling and invitation to life in Christ brought with it special blessings and privileges, which also meant it was a call to a radically different kind of life, one that could be recognized as distinctly Christlike.

Review 4:2.

1. True or false: The words in 4:2 inform the Ephesians of the most suitable vocation or ministry they should pursue.

The Ephesians were not called to a specific job because of their faith (although there would certainly be some jobs that would be off-limits to them). Instead, they were called to specific characteristics that would clearly demonstrate they had been called by God.

★ 2. **Using a Greek lexicon, look up these words from 4:2 and briefly summarize their meanings in your own words.**

Humility: ____

Gentleness: ______________________________________

Patience: ____

Bearing with: _____________________________________

Love: ____

Unlike we saw in Paul's letter to the Galatians, his letter to the Ephesians wasn't written with a specific "problem" in mind. For the most part, it seemed the churches in Ephesus were doing well. But Paul was well acquainted with the realities of the sinful human condition that persisted within him even after his conversion (Romans 7:15–20). And he knew this fallenness also existed within each member of the churches where he ministered.

That's why these characteristics were vital. After all, the call to "walk" means you might also trip, stumble, or fall. In those moments of sin, failure, tragedy, or pain, another believer's willingness to demonstrate humility and patience shines through.

★ 3. The Ephesians were called to be humble, gentle, patient, enduring, and loving. Are these characteristics present and growing in your life? In your church? Explain.

Review 4:3.

4. Circle the correct answer below. The Ephesians should eagerly maintain unity . . .

A. through sheer willpower.

B. found in the Spirit and with the Spirit's help.

C. but that was more of a backburner issue.

D. by praying and fasting.

The Holy Spirit establishes unity within the body of Christ. The Ephesians weren't responsible for *creating* unity—it already existed (2:14–18). But they were responsible for enthusiastically paying attention to unity and remaining at peace with one another through the empowerment of the Spirit.

Review 4:4–6.

5. How many times is the word *one* mentioned in this section?

Are you starting to see that Paul was passionate about unity? Here, Paul highlighted some of the things that united the early church. These core beliefs defined the Christian faith from the very beginning and still unite us today.

6. Match the phrases to their corresponding descriptions.

One body	Identification with Christ's death and resurrection
One Spirit	God the Father, the first person of the Trinity
One hope	Holy Spirit, the third person of the Trinity
One Lord	The expectation of Christ's return whereby all believers will reign with Him, receiving the promised inheritance
One faith	The object of faith is the person of Jesus Christ
One baptism	Jesus Christ, the second person of the Trinity
One God and Father of all	The church includes people from different ethnicities, social statuses, and families

All the "ones" Paul listed in these verses were—and are—statements of truth. These realities defined the early Christian faith and unified believers in Ephesus with believers in Rome, and all the Christians in between. These truths also unify us today. They remind us to eagerly maintain the unity, bought with a price and empowered by the Spirit, among those in our church, the church down the street, and the global church.

DAY 2

Ephesians 4:7–16

READ EPHESIANS 4:7–16

Review 4:7.

Diversity in the midst of unity is one of the beautiful realities of life in Christ. After all, God Himself is the perfect representation of this truth. God is one, yet each person of the Trinity—Father, Son, and Spirit—is unique.

The Ephesians were part of one body—the church—yet Christ had given each one a gift of grace. This grace doesn't refer to *saving* grace but instead to the grace that equips each Christian for life and work as a unique member of the body of Christ.

Review 4:8–10.

1. Write down the two words describing Christ's movement that are repeated in these verses. Beside them, write the number of times they're mentioned. Star the one that's repeated more often.

As we saw in 1:20–23, Christ is in His rightful place: seated at God's right hand in the heavenly places. But He did a little traveling before taking a seat.

This reference to Psalm 68 in Ephesians 4:8 evoked an image of God as the conqueror who, after receiving the spoils of war, gave gifts to His own people. Here, Paul presented Jesus graciously giving gifts to His church after conquering death and ruling over all.

Within Protestant denominations, there are three primary views of Christ's descent in 4:9–10. Some think this refers to Christ's incarnation—the time He spent on the earth. Others believe it specifically highlights His death on the cross, contrasted with His exaltation seen earlier in Ephesians. And still others believe this refers to Jesus going to gather the believing dead from a place referred to as "Abraham's bosom" (Luke 16:19–31 NKJV).

2. Which view makes the most sense to you? Use Scripture to support your answer.

Regardless of which view you picked, it's helpful to remember that Paul's emphasis is less on Christ's descent and more on Christ's ascension as the one who conquered "that He might fill all things."

Review 4:11–12.

There are a few spiritual gift lists found in Scripture (Romans 12:6–8; 1 Corinthians 12:1–11, 27–31; 1 Peter 4:11), and their contents vary, which likely means none of the lists are exhaustive. There is also diversity in who gives the gifts—sometimes it's God, other times it's the Holy Spirit, and here it's Christ. However, one thing remains consistent: The gifts are always to be used in service of others and for the benefit of the body of Christ. As *gifted* believers, we have the opportunity to follow the example of Jesus, who came not to be served but to serve (Matthew 20:26–28).

In writing to the Ephesians, Paul highlighted four gifts (maybe five—more to come on that) that relate to leadership within the church.

★ 3. **Use Bible study tools and 4:11–12 to fill in the table below.**

Leadership Gift	Role/Description	Goals
	One sent by God to be His messenger and commissioned by Jesus.	1.
Prophets	Responsible for communicating divine messages, exhorting, and encouraging within the church.	
	All Christians are called to share the good news (Matthew 28:18–20); however, this word referred to one within the church particularly skilled in evangelism.	2.
Shepherds/Teachers *(Note: This might be one gift, shepherd-teacher.)*		

Review 4:13–16.

The gifts and their purpose were all leading to one unified goal for believers.

4. Read 4:13 in the NLT and fill in the equation below summarizing Paul's end goal for the church.

leadership gifts + equipping/edifying the saints = ____________

As we saw in Galatians, false teaching was a serious problem for the early church. Even though the Ephesians weren't necessarily experiencing false teaching within their churches, Paul knew it was a possibility. Paul prepared them to combat false teaching by emphasizing unity around the "knowledge of the Son of God." The more the Ephesians learned and understood the truth, the more easily they could combat lies.

5. Describe the three images used in 4:14–16. What do you think Paul is trying to do with these images?

Christian maturity always starts and ends in love. The phrase "speaking the truth in love" might be familiar to you. And while the implications of this phrase could be demonstrated in the way Christians speak to one another, it's so much more than that. It's about living out the truth—truth in action, seen in all areas of a believer's life, including, but not limited to, speech.

★ 6. One theologian translated "speaking the truth in love" as "truthing in love."[1] How does this help you better understand Paul's point? What's one way you can live this out in the next week?

DAY 3

Ephesians 4:17–24

Review 4:17–19.

1. Reread 4:1. Compare and contrast Paul's language here with 4:17.

Paul continued his emphasis on truth, contrasting the current state of the unbelieving Gentiles with the holiness and purity to which the Ephesians were called.

The unbelieving Gentiles had hard hearts. The Greek word Paul used was *pōrōsis*, which can mean "calloused, blind, or stubborn"; it also relates to the process of petrification, in which organic matter turns to stone.[1] The reason for this hardness and willful rebellion was their own ignorance—a direct result of thinking consumed and controlled by lies.

★ 2. Paul expanded on this concept in his letter to the Romans. Read Romans 1:18–32 and write down the words or phrases that correlate with Paul's description of the Gentiles in Ephesians 4:17–18.

Futile minds/darkened understanding: ______________________

Alienated from God: ______________________

Ignorant: ______________________

Hard-hearted: ______________________

3. Use Ephesians 4:19 as a guide, and in your own words, summarize where this kind of thinking leads.

The walk of the Gentiles was filled with perversion, self-indulgence, debauchery, and a continual lust for evil. It's the opposite of a life in Christ that is lived in unity and marked by love, sacrifice, and long-suffering. Aren't you glad you are in Christ, invited to walk in truth?

Review 4:20–21.

We aren't snatched out of the world the moment we accept Christ as our Savior, but rather, we're called to live as light in the darkness. For newer Ephesian believers, the walk of the Gentiles might have felt like all-too-recent history. For others, the draw of their pre-Christ past might be a distant memory. Regardless, Paul wanted to remind the Ephesians that they had, in fact, learned a new way of life.

4. List the three phrases Paul used to describe how the Ephesians came to believe the "truth is in Jesus."

A. ______________________________

B. ______________________________

C. ______________________________

Review 4:22–24.

Paul gave two simple commands: "put off" and "put on." The Ephesians were to "dress themselves" appropriately given their new life in Christ. It's as if Paul instructed them to take off their "old-self togas" and put on their "new Christian togas."

5. Write down the command in 4:23.

This kind of renewal was not a one-time thing. Instead it was a daily practice—much like getting dressed. Every day as the Ephesians repeatedly reminded themselves of the truth they had learned about Christ and in Christ they would show the world they were wearing new clothes.

The new self—or new creation (2 Corinthians 5:17)—they were called to put on was in "the likeness of God." Every day, as the Ephesians dressed in their new selves, they would demonstrate the righteousness and holiness associated with God Himself to the pagan culture around them. Tomorrow we'll see some practical ways Paul envisioned them putting this into practice.

★ 6. List some ways you're currently renewing your mind and reminding yourself of the truth. (By the way, doing this Bible study definitely counts!)

DAY 4

Ephesians 4:25–29

READ EPHESIANS 4:25–29

1. Reread 4:24. What two characteristics did Paul use to describe the new self?

Putting on the new self meant living a life of integrity, a life characterized by right and true thinking. In this context, "righteousness" referred to *how* the Ephesians should think—and therefore live—because they *had already been made righteous* through Christ. Holy living represented their faithfulness to God and His commandments. Here, Paul gave some practical examples.

Review 4:25–27.

2. In your own words fill in the first two lines of the table below using 4:25–27. A few examples are already listed. (You'll complete the rest of the table later.)

Verse	Stop Doing This!	Start Doing This!	Why?
4:25			
4:26–27		It's okay to get angry, but watch yourself.	*Instead of providing a "why," Paul placed guardrails around anger.* A. Don't sin B. Don't let anger lead to bitterness or resentment C.
4:28			
4:29			

Paul didn't just tell the Ephesians what *not* to do. He showed them what new, righteous, and holy behaviors take the place of the behaviors he called them to eradicate.

"Be angry" shouldn't be read as a command to get angry. Instead, it was an expression that meant anger was allowed but should be kept under control.[1] Paul knew there was both righteous and unrighteous anger. For instance, Jesus was righteously angry when He threw the money changers out of the temple for taking advantage of the poor (Matthew 21:12–13).

God the Father, too, gets righteously angry (Jeremiah 30:23–24; Micah 7:18; Isaiah 61:8; Exodus 34:6) toward all the things that break His heart. There may have been times when you've experienced righteous anger toward those same things. It's also worth noting that God is *slow* to anger. And He calls us to be slow to anger too (James 1:19–20).

Paul's point in providing the additional caveats around anger was this: You aren't always the best judge of what's righteous, especially when you're mad. So to be people who exhibit self-control when angry, (a) don't sin in the midst of the emotion, (b) deal with the offense in a timely manner, and (c) don't give the devil an opportunity to tempt you.

★ 3. Briefly explain a time when you were righteously angry and a time when you were unrighteously angry. Is it hard to distinguish between the two? In what specific ways can you live out Paul's words when you get angry?

Review 4:28–29.

4. Using these verses, complete the last two lines of the table on page 191.

Paul encouraged the Ephesians to work hard so that every single one of them could be generous. This wasn't about a church tithe or a group donation (although those are important too). Rather, as individuals, they should be generous people who are ready to share.

The word *corrupting* in 4:29 comes from a Greek word that referred to rotten trees or fruit. Picture a moldy, squishy piece of old, brown fruit (don't forget the fruit flies buzzing around)—this was the kind of talk Paul was against.[2] In 4:25, Paul told the Ephesians to "speak the truth" to one another. Here, he emphasized another way of speaking—not in the rotten, vulgar, harmful way of the past, but in the new, righteous, and holy way. This kind of talk was encouraging, appropriate, and a blessing to anyone who heard it.

★ 5. **Look up *grace* (4:29) in a Greek lexicon, and write down what you find.** In what ways does this describe the way you talk to or about other believers? How would you like to grow in graceful speech?

Paul addressed speech in a few different ways, and you'll see this theme in Ephesians 5 as well. Here, as he unpacked some initial, practical ways the Ephesians should put on their new selves, he highlighted the impact words have on relationships—beginning with the way they affect the unity and health of Christ's body. It's hard to be unified if you're lying to one another.

Words reflect the state of your heart and mind (Luke 6:45), and they also influence your ability to love, forgive, enjoy, and relate to one another as brothers and sisters in Christ.

6. Write Psalm 19:14 below and ask God to do the same for you.

DAY 5

Ephesians 4:30–32

READ EPHESIANS 4:30–32

Review 4:30.

1. Use 4:30 to fill in the blanks below.

"_____ do not __________ the _______ __________ of God, by whom _____ were _________ for the day of _____________."

Because the word *and* connects 4:29 to 4:30, it's possible Paul wanted the Ephesians to make a direct connection between their speech and the grief it could bring to the Holy Spirit, emphasizing the power of the tongue (James 3:5–10). Even if Paul was highlighting this, it's clear that all the actions he previously mentioned—lying, unrighteous anger, stealing, and unwholesome speech (among many other things)—would cause the Holy Spirit pain. (And this is certainly not an exhaustive list, as we'll see in 4:31.)

Paul reminded the Ephesians of what he had written in 1:13–14: Believers are sealed with the Holy Spirit, marked as God's own, and guaranteed an inheritance. The presence of the Holy Spirit was proof that God's promise to make all things new on the final day of redemption was *as good as done*. It was set, even though they couldn't see it yet.

Even though the Ephesians' past had been dealt with (2:1–5) and their future was secure (1:14), they were responsible for how they lived during the in-between. Their lives—thoughts, words, and deeds—should not grieve God. They were His, and their walk should demonstrate that reality.

2. Ask the Holy Spirit to reveal anything in your life that is causing Him grief. Ask Him to help you put on the new self in this area. Use the space below to write a prayer of repentance, any specific changes you need to make, or the name of someone you need to ask to help keep you accountable.

Review 4:31.

★ 3. What six additional things did Paul tell the Ephesians to "put away" in 4:31? **Choose three to look up in a Greek lexicon and note what stands out to you.**

Paul added to the list of "old self" characteristics—things that grieve the Holy Spirit. Notice that he mentioned anger for the second time in Ephesians 4. This repetition is important given what we learned about anger on Day 4. Anger can often masquerade in our hearts as righteousness when it is actually unrighteous anger. When it's not properly dealt with, this anger leads to sin, violence, and harmful outbursts. Christians should pay close attention to their anger and—more often than not—put it away.

★ 4. What things make you angry the way Paul used the word in 4:31? (Hint: This is not righteous anger.) How can you "put away" this kind of anger? Explain.

Review 4:32.

Paul explained three more ways the Ephesians should relate to one another here, providing a bookend to his call for unity starting in 4:1–3.

5. Next to the bookends below, write the four characteristics Paul mentioned in 4:2 and the three he added in 4:32.

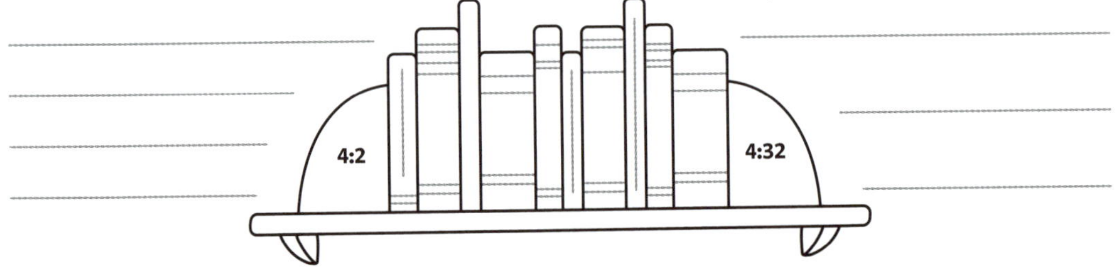

Paul called the Ephesians to forgive, which always feels easier to say than do. There would be times when someone in their church would act out of their "old self," causing pain and suffering to another. On the very day this letter was read to them, it's possible there were angry outbursts over breakfast or a vicious word quickly whispered behind another's back.

The command to be kind, compassionate, and forgiving still applies. And you can forgive, because "God in Christ forgave you."

Jesus—who never lied, never stole, and never slandered—gave Himself for the very people who not only did these things, but lusted after more and more evil. That's *every single one of us*. But God—in His mercy and according to His plan—saved us, made us alive, and adopted us.

Forgiveness is found in Him, and by His example we can forgive others. He's where the forgiveness is—*praise God*. And through His forgiveness of our sins, we've come to know that He's where the joy is!

6. What stood out to you most in this week's study? Why?

7. What did you learn or relearn about God and His character this week?

DAY 6

Corresponding Psalm & Prayer

1. What correlation do you see between Psalm 68 and this week's study?

2. What portions of this psalm stand out to you most?

3. Close by praying this prayer aloud:

Father,

Your name is the Lord*: Father of the fatherless and protector of widows. You went out before Your people, leading them through the* *wilderness, and the whole earth shook. And in Your great mercy, You rescued us from the depravity of our own sin. You daily bear us up, God of our salvation!*

I'm sorry for the times I've dressed myself as if You haven't given me a new life. I've lied, stolen, acted out of anger, and said vulgar things. I've given the enemy opportunities to tempt me, and I've given in to that temptation. Forgive me.

God, help me to "truth" in love. Jesus, show me how to maintain the unity in the church that You bought with Your blood. Spirit, lead me in Your way—the way of humility, gentleness, patience, and love.

I surrender my life to You, Lord—every moment of my day, each decision I make, I yield my will and way to Your perfect will and way.

I love You too. Amen.

DAY 7

Rest, Catch Up, or Dig Deeper

WEEKLY CHALLENGE

On Day 1, Paul urged the Ephesians to walk in a way that was worthy of God's calling. Humility, gentleness, patience, and bearing with one another in love were the characteristics that would display this walk to the world. On Day 5, he added three more characteristics to this list: kindness, compassion, and forgiveness. Jesus, as our perfect example, showed us how to live these out.

Choose one characteristic from this complete list and find a passage of Scripture where Jesus demonstrated it. Reflect on Jesus's example, pray, and think of a way you can practically display that same characteristic to someone else in the body of Christ this week!

WEEK 9

Ephesians 5

Scripture to Memorize

In all circumstances take up
the shield of faith, with
which you can extinguish
all the flaming darts
of the evil one . . .

Ephesians 6:16

DAILY BIBLE READING

Day 1: Ephesians 5:1–2

Day 2: Ephesians 5:3–14

Day 3: Ephesians 5:15–21

Day 4: Ephesians 5:22–24

Day 5: Ephesians 5:25–33

Day 6: Psalm 111

Day 7: Catch-Up Day

Corresponds to Day 350 of *The Bible Recap.*

WEEKLY CHALLENGE

See page 221 for more information.

DAY 1

Ephesians 5:1–2

Summarizing his teachings from Ephesians 4—on how believers should be unified as one family—Paul gave two practical action steps.

1. What two steps did Paul give for unity in the church? Fill in the blanks below.

A. Be ________________ of _________. (5:1)

B. And _________ in _________. (5:2)

Review 5:1.

In other places throughout the New Testament, early Christians are encouraged to imitate Christ and even to imitate Paul (as Paul imitated Christ). But this is the only imperative in the New Testament to imitate *God*.[1] So what does that look like? For that, we go to His Word.

★ 2. Look up each passage below and complete the table. The first row has been completed for you. In the last row, fill in your own example.

Scripture	What God Did	Who God Is	How I Can Imitate Him
Genesis 16:1–15	Saw Hagar—a hurting woman—and encouraged her	El Roi, the God who sees	Look for hurting people, and speak
Exodus 34:1–9			
Leviticus 14:21; Deuteronomy 15:7–11			

The Ephesian believers were "dearly loved children" (5:1 NIV), and so are we. Children are imitators by nature, watching their parents and caregivers to learn facial expressions, movements, and words. For better or worse, they learn by watching and imitating, so as they grow, they become more and more like the adults they watch.

When we watch our Father, we see that He is "gracious and merciful, slow to anger and abounding in steadfast love" (Psalm 145:8). And when we imitate Him, we become more and more like Him—gracious and merciful, slow to anger, and abounding in love.

Review 5:2.

Paul's second practical action step was to walk in love. And for this step, he told the Ephesians to look to the example set by God the Son, our older Brother—Jesus.

★ 3. How did Jesus walk in love? Write some of your favorite examples. Be specific.

Jesus taught the crowds, healed the sick, welcomed the outcasts, challenged the hypocrites, and forgave the sinners. Every action He took, every word He spoke, every step He made was done in love—perfect love. And when the time was right, He walked in love to a hill called Golgotha—carrying a cross He didn't deserve—to die in our place, sacrificing Himself for our sins.

Like the sacrifice Noah offered to God after the flood waters receded and the earth dried up (Genesis 8:13–22), Jesus's sacrifice was a "fragrant offering" to God. But unlike Noah's sacrifice, Jesus's was the *ultimate* sacrifice. Because He died and rose again, we live. Because He walked in perfect love, we also walk in love.

4. Write a prayer thanking Jesus for how He walked in love and asking God to help you imitate Him more.

DAY 2

Ephesians 5:3–14

READ EPHESIANS 5:3–14

After summarizing what the Ephesians should do—imitate God and walk in love—Paul spent some time explaining what they shouldn't do.

Review 5:3.

1. **Use a Greek lexicon to study the terms from 5:3 below.**

English Word or Phrase	Greek Word	Meanings
sexual immorality		
impurity		
covetousness		

★ 2. Did anything you learned surprise you?

Review 5:4–5.

For the saints at Ephesus who were called to be holy, even *joking* about sexual immorality, impurity, and covetousness was out of line. The Ephesians were certainly sinners, but because Christ had saved them, they were now saints. And saints don't treat heavy sins lightly. So what did Paul say they should do instead? Give thanks (5:4).

★ 3. How can thankfulness be an antidote to improper talk?

Until Jesus returned, the Ephesian saints—already-saved believers—were still sinners. Just like you, they would still be tempted by their old sin patterns, like sexual immorality, impurity, and covetousness. And sometimes they would fall to those temptations, finding themselves once again in need of repentance. But their sin was no longer what defined them. Just like you, they were saints, forgiven by God because of the work of Christ Jesus, and called to be holy. Paul encouraged them in the way of holy living, not because they would ever be able to prove themselves worthy of the salvation they'd already received, but because salvation changes everything.

Review 5:6–10.

God's children have no place partnering with those who are against Him. Paul didn't tell the Ephesians to avoid contact altogether with the "sons of disobedience," but to be distinct from them. They were to live out their calling as heirs.

4. Cross out the two words that shouldn't be in the statement below. Use 5:8 to guide you.

You were in darkness, but now you are in light in the Lord.

Because Jesus *is* the Light of the World (John 9:5), He makes believers light *in* the world, illuminating all that's good and right and true.

5. How was "try to discern" (5:10) translated in each Bible version below?

ESV	NIV	KJV	NLT	CSB
try to discern				

In each translation, the concept is the same: Discernment isn't a switch that's magically flipped on at the moment of salvation. Rather, discernment is a muscle that strengthens over time. The more you exercise it—through studying Scripture, praying, and living in Christian community—the stronger it becomes.

Review 5:11–14a.

There are times when believers will undoubtedly encounter "the unfruitful works of darkness," and must expose them to the light of Christ. But in doing so, they must not sin with gossip, slander, foolish talk, or crude jokes. Again, saints don't treat heavy sins lightly.

Review 5:14b.

Theologians have different thoughts about what Paul quoted here. It might have been a combination of several verses of Scripture.[1] It might have been a hymn or worship song that the Ephesians would have been familiar with.[2] It might have been a liturgy that was popular at the time.[3] Or it might have been a commonly held end-times understanding of the resurrection.[4]

So depending on what "it" was, the quotation's meaning could be the moment of salvation, when nonbelievers turn to Christ, which we call *justification*. Or it could mean the process by which believers learn to walk as children of light, which we call *sanctification*. Or it could mean the day when Jesus comes again and all things are made new, which we call *glorification*. But among these three possible meanings, there are two important similarities.

6. In 5:14b, what do believers do? What does Jesus do?

Believers	**Jesus Christ**

DAY 3

Ephesians 5:15–21

Having just told the Ephesian believers to "awake and arise"—or (depending on what source he quoted) that they had *already* woken and arisen, or that one glorious day they *would* awake and arise—Paul added a word of caution.

Review 5:15–16.

1. What reason did Paul give for the Ephesians making the best use of time? Why are the days evil? Use a study Bible or other study tool if you need help.

As we learned studying Galatians 1:4, Jesus had already delivered the Ephesians from the present evil age. But the results of His work weren't yet complete in their fullest, final form—and they still aren't. Theologians call this "the already and the not yet." So even while God uses these fleeting days to build His family and to banish sadness, these days are also marked by sin, which is why Paul called them evil. Time is a gift from God, and every minute He gives is an opportunity to join Him in the work He's doing and to "overcome evil with good" (Romans 12:21).

Review 5:17.

Unlike in 5:10—where discerning what is pleasing to the Lord was taught as a process—here, Paul gave an imperative: "Understand what the will of the Lord is." If that feels overwhelming, you're not alone. Surely some of the Ephesians felt the same way. So it's important to zoom out and look at some of the places in God's Word where His will is expressly defined for us.

2. Match each Scripture reference below to what it says about God's will.

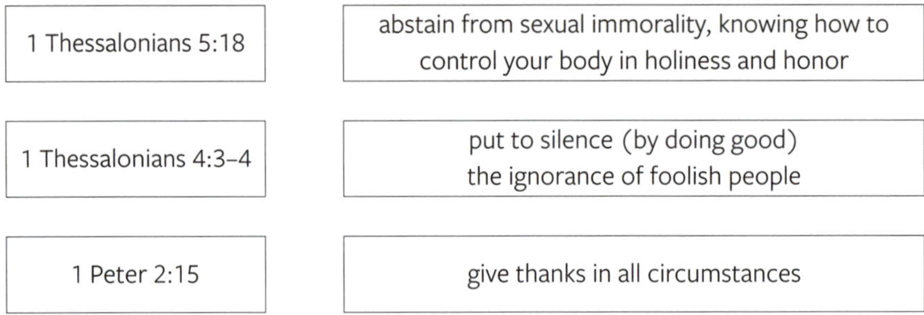

1 Thessalonians 5:18	abstain from sexual immorality, knowing how to control your body in holiness and honor
1 Thessalonians 4:3–4	put to silence (by doing good) the ignorance of foolish people
1 Peter 2:15	give thanks in all circumstances

Paul didn't tell the Ephesians what they should eat or which person they should marry or where they should build their homes. As we wisely and carefully walk in love and light, we will undoubtedly have choices to make. And when the will of the Lord seems unclear in those choices, we keep in mind the specific guidance He has given us, and we remember who He is and what He loves. And for the details? We pray like the psalmist, "Teach me to do your will, for you are my God! Let your good Spirit lead me on level ground!" (Psalm 143:10).

Review 5:18–20.

While debauchery—extreme indulgence or excess—leads to sickness and ruin, being filled with the Spirit leads to something entirely different.

★ 3. According to 5:19, how should Spirit-filled people speak to one another? What should happen in our hearts?

Like when he contrasted sexual immorality and thanksgiving (5:4), Paul's contrast of drunkenness and music may seem disconnected at first. But consider this: While drunkenness is self-focused, these types of songs are Spirit-led. Drunkenness is a waste of time and resources, but this type of music is an investment of both. Drunkenness has a destructive impact on the body, and praise has an edifying impact on the soul (*and* the body). Drunkenness is a temporary pleasure that could lead to lifelong heartache, but making music for the Lord is an eternal posture that leads to everlasting joy. And it's worth noting that thanksgiving is also a part of this (5:20).

Review 5:21.

Wrapping up this section, Paul introduced an idea that he expanded on in the following verses.

4. **Use a Greek lexicon to define *submit* from 5:21.** Write what you learn.

This word is used thirty-eight times in the New Testament (twenty-three of those instances were written by Paul), yet the topic of submission is often misunderstood and sadly misrepresented. We'll dive deeper into this tomorrow, but before we do, let's reflect on the framework laid out in 5:21.

★ 5. What reason did Paul give here for submitting to one another? Why is that important?

DAY 4

Ephesians 5:22–24

READ EPHESIANS 5:22–24

Back in 5:21, Paul directed the Ephesian church to submit—*hypotassō*—to one another. Here, using the same word, he instructed one group of Ephesians in particular.

1. Let's review. What does the word *submit—hypotassō*—mean? Go back to your answer from Day 3, prompt 4 if you need a reminder.

Before we dig in, it's important to acknowledge that throughout the history of the church, these verses have, at times, been shamefully used to defend some husbands' sins. And throughout the history of the church, these verses have, at times, been willfully ignored to excuse some wives' sins. It's also important to keep in mind that we should not use this passage alone to form an entire theology on the roles of men and women. These verses certainly do help to inform that theology, but they're only one car of the complete train. Our job today—whether you are a man or a woman, and whether you are single or married—is to study these verses faithfully, learning about God's heart for order, honor, and love.

Review 5:22.

2. What specific instruction did Paul give the Ephesians in 5:22?

   A. All women, submit to all men.

   B. Husbands, submit to your own wives.

   C. Wives, submit to your own husbands.

★ 3. What did Paul compare this submission to? Why is that important?

In first-century Ephesus, Greco-Roman household codes of conduct were commonly used to outline roles and responsibilities for a household's members. They were so widely used at the time that these secular codes were likely shaping Christian marriages more than Christ Himself was.[1] So Paul included a Christ-centered household code of conduct in his letter to the Ephesians.

If "wives, submit to your own husbands" sounds to your modern ears like what you'd expect from the first century, consider this: Ancient near-eastern cultures insisted that women know their place both at home *and* in society. Their compliance was expected and their obedience was demanded—not just to their husbands, but to *all* men. But Paul instructed wives to submit specifically to their own husbands. What's more, he dignified them with the example he gave: Jesus Christ and His church.

Review 5:23.

4. Complete the analogy statement below.

   The ____________ is the _______ of the _______ _______ as ________ is the _______ of the _______.

Marriage is a covenant relationship designed to mirror the covenant between Christ and His church. Throughout this passage, Paul taught the Ephesians that there is order and authority in Christian households. But make no mistake—a higher level of responsibility or authority does not mean a higher level of value. If you need a reminder of what Paul taught about the value and dignity of every person in Christ's church, go back and reread Galatians 3:28.

In a Christian marriage, both spouses are equally valued and cherished as God's children. The heart of this passage is describing the ideal; it isn't suggesting that wives (or husbands, for that matter) should remain in unsafe spaces. Throughout Scripture, God condemns those who wield power to dominate the vulnerable (Psalm 9:18; Isaiah 3:14–15; Amos 2:7; Mark 9:42).*

Review 5:24.

The church willingly and joyfully submits to her Savior, who loved her so completely that He gave Himself up for her. Christ wants the church to grow and thrive under His care (Matthew 16:18; Matthew 28:19–20; John 10:10).

In a Christian marriage, the wife is meant to willingly and joyfully submit to her husband, who loves her so selflessly that he would give himself up for her. The husband should want his wife to grow and thrive under his care (more on this tomorrow).

So unlike Greco-Roman household codes, this relationship is designed to be marked by selflessness, trust, protection, and joy.

★ 5. What did you learn about Paul's instructions to Ephesian wives today? What questions do you still have about this text (if any)?

* If you are in such a marriage, you must seek help from the leadership of your local church and/or other local authorities.

DAY 5

Ephesians 5:25–33

In a Greco-Roman household code, instructions for husbands would have been short, something like *You're in charge of the household and everyone in it—make sure they know.* But with four verses instructing wives and ten verses instructing husbands, Paul radically redefined the role of a Christian husband—not just with the length of his instructions but with the content. For the Christian husband, being "the head of the wife" (5:23) isn't about oppressive dominance, but sacrificial love.[1]

Review 5:25–28.

1. True or false: Paul taught the Ephesians here how all men should interact with all women.

Speaking to husbands, Paul began his instructions by reminding them of what Christ did for the church.

★ 2. In 5:26–27, what three purposes are named as the reasons Christ gave Himself up for the church?

A. That He might

____

____

B. That He might

____

____

C. That she might

____

____

The sacrificial love that Christ gave His church came *first*. Only then was the church made holy, able to present herself to Him "in splendor, without spot or wrinkle or any such thing." In other words, His love for her makes her lovely. In the same way, Paul taught that husbands must sacrificially love their wives *first*. The husband's selfless and sacrificial love for his wife makes her lovely.

It's worth adding a note here to single women: Choose carefully. As hard and lonely as singleness can be, being married to a man who doesn't model Christ's sacrificial love will be much harder and much lonelier. And for single men? Choose carefully. As hard and lonely as singleness can be, being married to a woman who doesn't model the church's submission to Christ will be much harder and much lonelier.

Review 5:29–30.

3. What happens when someone neglects to nourish and cherish their body? How does this relate to a husband's love for his wife?

4. What are some practical ways that a husband can nourish his marriage and cherish his wife?

Review 5:31–32.

Like Paul did in 5:31, Jesus also quoted Genesis 2:24 when teaching His disciples about marriage (Matthew 19:5; Mark 10:7). By going all the way back to the garden of Eden, we see that God's design for marriage was introduced before the fall. After the fall, Paul taught here, the design still stands, and Christ fulfilled and redeemed that design in His perfect love for the church.

Christian marriage is an opportunity for both husbands and wives to mirror the relationship between Christ and His church. They get to paint a picture of the mystery God has been revealing all along—that because of Him, we are one. The wife has the honor—and the challenge—of submitting to her husband joyfully. And the husband has the privilege—and the challenge—of loving his wife selflessly.

Review 5:33.

5. In 5:33, how did Paul summarize 5:22–32?

Husbands—

Wives—

If you're a married person whose spouse doesn't strive to model Christ or His church, these last two days of study may have been distinctly painful. In a similar way, if you're a single person who longs for a spouse, these last two days of study may have been particularly challenging. Be encouraged by what the apostle John wrote: "God is greater than our heart[s], and he knows everything" (1 John 3:20). Your worth is found in the one whose image you bear, and it is Christ Himself who makes you lovely. His love for you is perfect, and He's where the joy is!

6. What stood out to you most in this week's study? Why?

★ 7. What did you learn or relearn about God and His character this week?

DAY 6

Corresponding Psalm & Prayer

READ PSALM 111

1. What correlation do you see between Psalm 111 and this week's study?

2. What portions of this psalm stand out to you most?

3. Close by praying this prayer aloud:

Father,

Your works are great, full of splendor and majesty. Your righteousness endures forever! You are holy and awesome, remembering

Your covenant forever. You are gracious and merciful, sending redemption to Your people.

You called me to imitate You, but I've imitated the fallen world instead. You called me to walk in love, but I've walked in anger, jealousy, and bitterness. I've been sexually immoral, impure, covetous, and debaucherous. I've treated my heavy sins lightly. I repent, and I turn back to You.

Teach me to fear You, as the beginning of wisdom. Remind me to give thanks always. Lead me in singing songs, hymns, and spiritual songs. And as I imitate You, make me more like You—gracious and merciful, slow to anger, and abounding in love. As I walk in love, make my words and my actions reflect who You are.

I surrender my life to You, Lord—every moment of my day, each decision I make, I yield my will and way to Your perfect will and way.

I love You too. Amen.

DAY 7

Rest, Catch Up, or Dig Deeper

WEEKLY CHALLENGE

On Day 2, you learned that thankfulness is an antidote to improper talk (5:4). Every day this week, write down three things you're thankful for. Every day, share at least one of those things with someone in an effort to fill your speech with thanksgiving and praise!

WEEK 10

Ephesians 6

Scripture to Memorize

. . . and take the helmet of salvation, and the sword of the Spirit, which is the word of God, praying at all times in the Spirit, with all prayer and supplication.

Ephesians 6:17–18a

DAILY BIBLE READING

Day 1: Ephesians 6:1–4
Day 2: Ephesians 6:5–9
Day 3: Ephesians 6:10–13
Day 4: Ephesians 6:14–20
Day 5: Ephesians 6:21–24
Day 6: Psalm 27
Day 7: Catch-Up Day

Corresponds to Day 350 of *The Bible Recap*.

WEEKLY CHALLENGE

See page 245 for more information.

DAY 1

Ephesians 6:1–4

READ EPHESIANS 6:1–4

Review 6:1.

In last week's study, we examined 5:21–33 with cultural context in mind. Paul was both mirroring and counterculturally turning Greco-Roman household codes on their head. He does the same thing in today's passage.

The fact that Paul addressed children directly was countercultural in and of itself. It indicated that they were worthy of direct conversation amid a gathering of adults. And it indicated that what they did mattered. Much like we saw with Paul's treatment of women and marriage in his letters, this was actually an *elevation* of children.

1. Fill in the key phrase from 6:1 below.

   "Children, obey your parents ____ ______ _______, for this is right."

What an invitation to freedom here. Some children have terrible earthly parents. And much like the slaves Paul will address on Day 2, and much like the way Paul encouraged Christians to live under governing authorities (Romans 13:1–5), these children were invited to obey their parents "in the Lord." In Colossians 3:23–24 (NIV), Paul wrote, "Whatever you do, work at it with all your heart, as working for the Lord, not for human masters, since you know that you will receive an inheritance from the Lord as a reward. It is the Lord Christ you are serving." Whether these children had good parents or bad ones, they had a good Father in heaven—it was the Lord Christ they were serving.

2. In 5:1, how did Paul tell the Ephesians to be imitators of God?

In a healthy, loving parent/child relationship, a parent teaches the child obedience so that the child will grow up knowing how to obey even when they don't understand or don't want to understand. In that way, all Christians—as children of God—can take a lesson from this.

Review 6:2–3.

This reference to Exodus 20:12 comes from the Ten Commandments, which the Lord gave to Moses and the Israelites in the wilderness. In this agrarian culture, being able to "live long in the land" was directly tied to a family's ability to live in harmony with one another and pass down the land and its responsibilities to future generations. In other words, this promise not only makes sense, but also reminds us of the joys of obedience.

Many of God's commands challenge us to a higher calling—a perseverance in trials, a willingness to forgo earthly pleasure for the sake of the gospel, for the sake of the "something better" God has planned for us beyond this life (Hebrews 11:40). But *this* commandment came with a promise, and it serves as a reminder that obeying God also brings life more abundantly here on earth (John 10:10).

★ 3. Describe a time when God called you to do something you didn't understand in the moment. Can you think of a time afterward when you were able to see the wisdom or fruit of your obedience?

Review 6:4.

The fact that this verse was directed specifically to fathers was *absolutely revolutionary*—it was so outside the bounds of this culture. In the Greco-Roman household codes, fathers were given authority over their children. They weren't told they had a responsibility *to* them.

The phrase "bring them up" comes from an ancient Greek word that typically described bodily nourishment, like the way Christ is described as feeding and taking care of the church in Ephesians 5:29. Paul told these fathers that roles such as nurturing, relational tending, teaching, and disciplining aren't solely left to the mothers or the church. Fathers, bring up your children.

As Paul taught these countercultural truths to the Ephesians, he also left us with meaningful implications for our own lives—not just as they apply to our earthly families but as they apply to our relationship with our heavenly Father as well.

★ 4. What have you learned about the character of God your Father that makes it easier for you to trust and obey Him?

DAY 2

Ephesians 6:5–9

READ EPHESIANS 6:5–9

Throughout the New Testament, Paul encouraged these early church members to persevere in ways that emulated Christ in *whatever* circumstance they found themselves. He spoke to wives and husbands, the highly educated and the illiterate, kings and kids. And to all of them, he pointed to Jesus and basically said, "*This way of life is available today. You don't have to wait for your circumstances to change in order to live in the freedom of Christ Jesus.*" That is our miraculous invitation.

That being said, this passage has been misunderstood at times—and even purposely misused—to support the erroneous idea that Paul approved of slavery. On the contrary, Paul was merely addressing a system that existed, not endorsing that system.

★ 1. What in Luke 4:18 (in which Jesus quoted Isaiah 61's prophecy about Him) helps clarify this? How do Jesus's words about why He came affect your heart, especially regarding slavery?

Review 6:5.

Paul had personally experienced many of the sufferings we might associate with slavery when we hear the term. He was whipped, beaten with rods, pelted with stones, transported in ships as a prisoner, and deprived of sleep, food, and water, and left cold and naked (2 Corinthians 11:23–27). Paul didn't write this letter from a comfy office desk; he wrote it while in chains (6:20).

Bear that in mind as you read this passage. And now, hear the boldness in Paul's Holy Spirit–inspired words from our God who sees and who also was beaten, was imprisoned, was spit on, felt forsaken, and was put to death (Matthew 27:27–50) for our *eternal* and better freedom that can never be taken away.

2. Fill in this key phrase in 6:5.

"... obey your earthly masters with fear and trembling, with a sincere heart, ___ _____ _________ _________."

3. What phrase does this remind you of from Day 1's study? (Hint: check out 6:1.)

When you see the word *slavery*, perhaps you think of the brutalities committed against slaves in the more recent past. Slavery in this Greco-Roman culture, however, was sometimes more akin to employment, like a long-term job within a household. Sometimes (though not always) that even implied certain levels of security. Throughout the history of the world, slaves of all sorts have endured evils and atrocities that grieve the heart of God (Exodus 3:7–8; James 5:4).

Remember that this was a letter. It would have been read among the whole congregation, in front of masters and slaves, standing together in the same church gathering. There's a note of defiance here that would have stood out. God essentially says to slaves: *"Don't look at your masters; look at Me. I have called you by name. You are Mine"* (see Isaiah 43:1).

4. On Day 1, we read Colossians 3:23–24. Reread it now. What does this passage promise?

Review 6:6–8.

★ 5. What do you think the phrase "eye-service" might mean? Can you think of an example of it in your own life? If so, describe.

In 6:5, Paul had reminded slaves that it was really the Lord Christ they were serving. That was an invitation to freedom and dignity for all those who were living under bad earthly masters. In essence, Paul said, "*You have dignity and honor, because God is your boss. When you go to work, you're walking into your Dad's office. You are sons and daughters of the boss of the universe.*" But 6:6 reminded them that this boss didn't walk in and out of the room. Proverbs 15:3 says, "The eyes of the LORD are in every place, keeping watch on the evil and the good." What an encouragement to the righteous. And what a warning to the devious who change their behavior in secret—masters included.

It's possible to please men and displease the Lord. These Ephesians were being warned that people-pleasing wasn't the goal. Looking like a good worker only to please the boss when the boss was in the room was not service to the Lord. And God promises that our service to the Lord will be rewarded.

Review 6:9.

6. Who did Paul say had the same ultimate boss?

Masters in this culture would have certainly been thought of (or at least would've thought of themselves) as superior to slaves in the hierarchy of the day. But Paul said they all had equal footing in the eyes of the Lord—and equal obligation to each other to treat one another as servants of Christ. Look at Paul planting those seeds that so obviously undermine the very foundations of slavery—even as he graciously encouraged those suffering under it in the meantime, and even as he was both a leader to them and in chains.

DAY 3

Ephesians 6:10–13

READ EPHESIANS 6:10–13

Review 6:10.

1. With what word or phrase does Paul begin today's passage?

   A. "Anyway"
   B. "In other news"
   C. "Finally"
   D. "So . . . new topic!"

The armor of God may be a familiar concept, but today we'll begin to look at it in its full context. Paul's "finally" reminds us that everything he was about to say was based on all the groundwork he'd previously laid in this letter to the Ephesians. So as we begin to wrap up this book and head to the big finale, let's review. What have we learned about who God is and what He's afforded to us through His life, death, resurrection, and ascension and through the power of the Spirit?

2. Respond to the questions in this overview of Ephesians 1–3, as it relates to our preparation for today's study.

Ephesians 1	In 1:4, Paul reminded the Ephesians they were chosen by God in Christ when?	
Ephesians 2	According to 2:2, in the past, the Ephesians were dead, serving who?	
Ephesians 3	In 3:16, Paul prayed the Ephesians would be strengthened in what, and with what?	

In 3:13–21, Paul prayed a prayer for the Ephesians with such grand language that it may take us a second to step back and remember that the things Paul described are real and are afforded to us as believers: "Now to him who is able to do far more abundantly than all that we ask or think . . ." Imagine a military general on a horse riding before troops—it's a prayer that almost feels like a battle cry. Perhaps that's precisely what Paul had in mind. . . .

3. What does Paul say to be strong in?

If Ephesians 1–3 was about laying the groundwork of the glorious truths we're afforded through faith in Christ, then Ephesians 4–6 was Paul's encouragement on how to apply that truth. In Ephesians 4, the Ephesians were encouraged to grow in maturity. And Ephesians 5–6 moved into instructions on how to live in unity, bearing the deeper truths in mind. Paul told them not to be deceived by the world's darkened way of perceiving reality: "Wake up" (5:14 NIV)!

Why? *Because we're at war.*

Review 6:11–12.

We will have troubles in this life. Jesus told us this.

★ 4. Why did Jesus say to "take heart" in John 16:33? Why is this a comfort to us? Explain.

In 1 Peter 4:12, we're told not to be surprised by fiery trials "as though something strange were happening to you." We should expect trials. Don't treat them as a shock. "You *will* have trouble." We *are* at war.

You may assume any reference to spiritual powers of darkness always implies some kind of paranormal activity. But don't be deceived: The enemies of God may also aim to "devour" you (1 Peter 5:8) through things like impatience, pride, deceit, irritation, or even how the barista messed up your order in such an infuriating way that you're barely able to share the gospel with the person you came to meet.

Some believers think of wars against darkness as something that happens "against flesh and blood"—culture wars, for example. But spiritual wars are far more likely to happen in your own heart, in your own home, in your own intolerance. One of the great deceptions of the enemy is to convince us we aren't at war, that our daily indiscretions don't matter.

5. What Paul told the Ephesians they wrestle against is true for us today too. Write *I* in the first blank, then fill in the other blanks with truths from 6:12.

"For __ do not wrestle against flesh and blood, but against _____ ________, against _____ ________________, against _____ ________ ________ _______ _______ _________ __________, against ___ _______ _________ ___ _______ ___ _____ ______________ _________."

Everyone on earth is fighting a spiritual war, whether they know it or not. And notice how Paul listed these spiritual forces—they're organized, like military ranks. We're meant to know this, but we're not meant to fear it.

According to Ephesians 1:19–23, Jesus isn't the opposite of these principalities—He's *over* them. They are under His feet.

★ 6. One great verse to memorize and pray aloud when you're afraid is 1 Corinthians 15:24. Write it in all caps below. Then list a few specific ways it impacts your confidence amid spiritual battles.

Review 6:13.

Therefore, because we are at war, we (and the Ephesians) must take up the whole armor of God "to stand firm."

We'll unpack all that implies in tomorrow's study. But as you go out today, remember that you are God's workmanship (2:10), His *poiēma* as it's called in the Greek—also the root word of *poem*. We're His epic battle poem He wrote long ago, and we already know the ending.

Now, go have a great day at war!

DAY 4

Ephesians 6:14–20

READ EPHESIANS 6:14–20

Review 6:14–17.

Paul listed the armor in the order a soldier would have put it on. The Ephesians were familiar with this armor. But for modern readers, here are clues to help us understand the richness of what Paul was illustrating:

- Belts in Roman armor weren't like a belt you might think of today. They were leather tunics that ran from the midsection all the way down to the upper thighs. They were a unifying piece into which other pieces were tucked and held together.
- A breastplate was strapped onto the chest and remained on throughout battle—it didn't come off.
- The shields of that day were large—like, the size of a door—so a line of soldiers working and walking together with their shields could become a wall.
- A soldier's shoes were often studded with nails, much like cleats, which allowed for a firmer grip on the foundation, even in quick movements.
- The only significant area uncovered by armor was the soldier's back. This was because Roman soldiers fought back-to-back—the phrase "I've got your back" taking on a literal meaning.

1. In the diagram on the next page, label each piece of armor listed in 6:14–17.

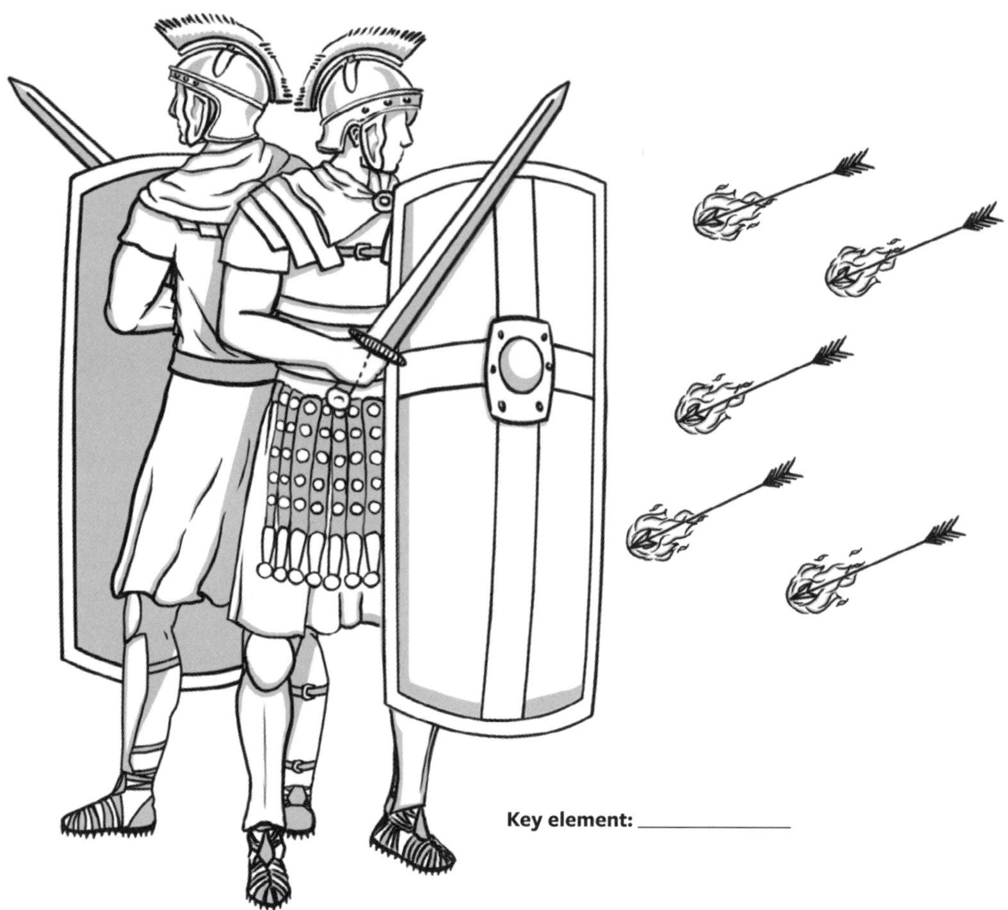

2. Which context clues give you a better understanding of the armor and what we're invited into in Christ? How can you apply the concept of the soldiers fighting back-to-back to your own life?

Stand therefore, having put *all* this on. And Paul reiterated this in 1 Thessalonians 5:8—to put on "for a helmet the hope of salvation."

3. What truths about the hope of our salvation could you write on your helmet to protect your mind from discouragement? Write them on the armor diagram now.

Note that the breastplate of righteousness is not a righteousness dependent on our own works or perfection—*praise God!* That breastplate of righteousness is Christ's righteousness imputed to us by His work on the cross (Galatians 2:15–16). And the shield of faith we take up is not faith in our own abilities or strength—it's faith in Christ, who has already won the victory.

However, we are told to *take up* our faith—which means we can choose to use or not use the faith we have any time we face the attacks of the enemy. When we use our faith against the enemy's attacks, God promises victory!

★ 4. Label the fiery darts in the diagram with some accusations you think the enemy might try to use against you. Then write below what "taking up" your shield of faith might look like in the face of those particular accusations.

Review 6:18–20.

Notice the armor is incomplete without prayer. The sentence describing the helmet and sword flows right into a description of prayer.

5. Go back to your diagram and label prayer as a key element of the armor.

"With all prayer and supplication" can also be translated as "with all kinds of prayer" (NIV)—prayer sung, prayer whispered, prayer shouted, prayer kneeling, prayer standing, prayer running, prayer alone, prayer together, *prayer for each other*. Why? Because this is not a solo mission.

Remember, Paul was imprisoned in Rome when he wrote this. But instead of asking for prayer that he'd be released, he requested prayer for boldness to proclaim the gospel. It was his boldness that had gotten him arrested in the first place, yet his prayer request was for *more boldness*. He may have been preparing for his upcoming encounter with Caesar.

★ 6. It may not seem as though Paul lacked boldness. Why do you think he requested prayer for that?

Paul called himself an "ambassador in chains." And though he perhaps was literally shackled, there's also a deeper meaning here. This Greek word could also be translated to mean the gold chains ambassadors or dignitaries wore at the time to evidence the dignity, authority, and splendor of the government they represented. What a flex! Paul was essentially saying, *"I wear the armor of the Most High God. And these chains are the jewelry of the King of the universe."*

DAY 5

Ephesians 6:21–24

READ EPHESIANS 6:21–24

Review 6:21–22.

Paul ended this letter by telling the Ephesians that Tychicus (pronounced TIH-kuh-kuhs) would deliver it in person, so he could fill them in on how Paul was doing while imprisoned in Rome. Notice this cast keeps growing. As we learned on Day 4—but really, throughout all of Ephesians—*this is not a solo mission*. In Paul's letters, we see repeated names like Barnabas, Silas, Timothy, Priscilla . . . and now add Tychicus. Though Paul was greatly used by God in the early church, never forget the beauty of the church God was building—and how focused Paul was on supporting that "community unity." He never stopped talking about it. We need each other.

Tychicus was mentioned as a faithful and trustworthy colaborer many times throughout Paul's ministry (Acts 20:4; Colossians 4:7; 2 Timothy 4:12; Titus 3:12). And in many of the mentions, he's depicted as a deliverer of Paul's messages, both verbal and written. But lest we imagine Tychicus driving across town or cc'ing the churches in an email, it's helpful to remember that Paul wrote this letter to the Ephesians while he was under house arrest in Rome more than eight hundred miles away.

1. On the map below, draw a line to track Tychicus's journey from Rome to Ephesus.

Traveling from Rome to Ephesus was no small journey. And long journeys at that time were not easy—they took months. On top of that, journeys by sea always had the potential to be life-threatening. Ancient history is full of shipwreck stories. Paul himself experienced a wreck in Acts 27. The fact that Paul so badly wanted to encourage the Ephesians that he was willing to send Tychicus across the sea to do it says something about the power of encouragement and the importance of words.

★ 2. Have you ever discounted the value of encouragement, perhaps dismissing it as fluff that only weak people need? If so, describe. What have you learned about Paul and the early church that challenges that view?

Paul took care with his encouragements. They were specific, thoughtful, powerful, and full of an expectation that they would produce results. Paul knew the Ephesians wouldn't be able to persevere without encouragement. They were living the kinds of lives that required it.

3. What is the root word of *encouragement*? What does that tell you about encouragement's ability to promote action?

4. Who could you encourage today? What would it look like to encourage them specifically?

★ 5. Who do you need to ask for encouragement from? Or who have you received encouragement from lately, and what was its effect?

Review 6:23–24.

Paul began this letter to the Ephesians with "grace and peace." And he ended it with the same—this letter about unity in the body, "being joined together" (2:21), and, well, getting along.

Paul knew his readers would continue to need encouragement to the end of their days—they would never reach perfection on this side of eternity. But he brought this letter to its finale with a beautiful reminder: The love we have in Jesus is "love incorruptible." This phrase in the Greek refers to a love we have in Christ that will never die or decay or become less. Perfect, endless, unruined love—what a Savior! He's where the joy is!

6. What stood out to you most in this week's study? Why?

7. What did you learn or relearn about God and His character this week?

DAY 6

Corresponding Psalm & Prayer

READ PSALM 27

1. What correlation do you see between Psalm 27 and this week's study?

2. What portions of this psalm stand out to you most?

3. Close by praying this prayer aloud.

Father,

You are my light and my salvation—I fear only You. You are my refuge—I don't have to be afraid.

You've taught me, Your beloved child, how to obey You. But I've stubbornly gone my own way, abandoning Your goodness. I am Your adopted child, and Your Son Jesus was forsaken for my freedom. But I've willfully disobeyed You, ignoring Your sacrifice.

Teach me Your way, and lead me on a level path. Remind me of the incorruptible love of Jesus. Like Paul, I ask that You give me boldness for You—no matter what trials may come. And like David, I ask to dwell in Your house and gaze upon Your beauty forever.

I believe that I will look upon Your goodness while I'm still here in the land of the living! So I surrender my life to You, Lord—every moment of my day, each decision I make, I yield my will and way to Your perfect will and way.

I love You too. Amen.

DAY 7

Rest, Catch Up, or Dig Deeper

WEEKLY CHALLENGE

In light of our study of the armor of God, be mindful of the battle you face (and that He has already won). Every morning as you get dressed for the day, pray through Ephesians 6:10–20 aloud. Put on that armor of God and expect to use it. Remember, as Christians, we're fighting a battle that's already been won by Christ—*that's* the righteousness we wear on our chest. Now, go have a great week at war!

FOR GROUP LEADERS

Thank you for using this study and leading others through it as well! Each week has a wide variety of content (daily Bible reading, content and questions, Scripture memorization, weekly challenge, and resources) to help the reader develop a range of spiritual disciplines. Feel free to include as much or as little of that in your meetings as you'd like. The details provided in How to Use This Study (pp. 7–9) will be helpful to you and all your group members, so be sure to review that information together!

It's up to you and your group how you'd like to structure your meetings, but we suggest including time for discussion of the week's study and Bible text, mutual encouragement, and prayer. You may also want to practice your Scripture memory verses together as a group or in pairs. As you share with each other, "consider how to stir up one another to love and good works" (Hebrews 10:24) and "encourage one another and build one another up" (1 Thessalonians 5:11).

Here are some sample questions to help facilitate discussion. This is structured as a weekly study, but if your group meets at a different frequency, you may wish to adjust the questions accordingly. Cover as many questions as time allows, or feel free to come up with your own. And don't forget to check out the additional resources we've linked for you at MyDGroup.org/Resources/GalEph.

Sample Discussion Questions

What questions did this week's study or Bible text bring up for you?

What stood out to you in this week's study?

What did you notice about God and His character?

How were you challenged by your study of the Bible text? Is there anything you want to change in light of what you learned?

How does what you learned about God affect the way you live in community?

What correlation did you see between the psalm from Day 6 and this week's study of Galatians (or Ephesians)?

Have you felt God working in you through the weekly challenge? If so, how?

Is your love for God's Word increasing as we go through this study? If so, how?

Did anything you learned increase your joy in knowing Jesus?

ACKNOWLEDGMENTS

Laura Buchelt, Emily Pickell, Abbey Dane, Emma Dotter, Kirsten McCloskey, and Liz Suggs—thank you for your incredible research, creativity, wisdom, humility, and laughter. It's truly a *blast* to study God's Word with you all!

Olivia Le—thank you for making our writing summits so seamless and for bringing levity to our lunches.

Lisa Jackson—you continue to be such a gift as a guide, agent, and friend.

And to the rest of the incredible D-Group Team—Rachel Mantooth, Lindsay Ruhter, Warwick Fuller, Jane Long, Meg Mitchell, Evaline Asmah, and our board, leaders, members, and church partners around the world—I love being on mission with you!

NOTES

Week 1: Day 1

1. “What Is an Apostle?” Got Questions, https://www.gotquestions.org/what-is-an-apostle.html.
2. *The Holy Bible, English Standard Version* (Crossway, 2001), 972n1.

Week 1: Day 2

1. “Galatians 1 – Challenging a Different Gospel,” Enduring Word, https://enduringword.com/bible-commentary/galatians-1/.

Week 1: Day 5

1. “Galatians 1 – Challenging a Different Gospel,” Enduring Word, https://enduringword.com/bible-commentary/galatians-1/.

Week 3: Day 1

1. “Galatians 3 – The Christian, Law, and Living by Faith,” Enduring Word, https://enduringword.com/bible-commentary/galatians-3/.

Week 3: Day 3

1. *ESV Women’s Study Bible* (Crossway, 2020), 1925.

Week 3: Day 4

1. See “Galatians 3 – The Christian, Law, and Living by Faith,” Enduring Word, https://enduringword.com/bible-commentary/galatians-3/ and *ESV Women’s Study Bible* (Crossway, 2020), 1925n3:19.

Week 3: Day 5

1. Martin Luther, “Galatians Three by Martin Luther,” Blue Letter Bible, last modified June 27, 2005, https://www.blueletterbible.org/Comm/luther_martin/Gal/Gal003.cfm.
2. “Galatians 3 – The Christian, Law, and Living by Faith,” Enduring Word, https://enduringword.com/bible-commentary/galatians-3/.
3. “G5207 - huios – Strong’s Greek Lexicon (ESV),” Blue Letter Bible, accessed March 25, 2025, https://www.blueletterbible.org/lexicon/g5207/esv/mgnt/0-1/, *ESV Women’s Study Bible* (Crossway, 2020), 1926n3:26.

Week 3: Day 7

1. Ligonier Editorial, “The Threefold Use of the Law,” Ligonier, August 21, 2015, https://learn.ligonier.org/articles/threefold-use-law; *Luther’s Small Catechism with Explanation* (Concordia Publishing House, 2011), 97.

Week 4: Day 3

1. John Stott, *The Message of Galatians*, rev. ed. (InterVarsity Press, 2020), 87.

Week 4: Day 4

1. "Allegory," Poetry Foundation, https://www.poetryfoundation.org/education/glossary/allegory.
2. This question is based on the one posed in John Stott, *The Message of Galatians* (InterVarsity Press, 2020), 97.

Week 5: Day 1

1. Dallas Willard, *The Great Omission: Reclaiming Jesus's Essential Teachings on Discipleship* (HarperCollins, 2006), 34.

Week 5: Day 5

1. "Galatians 6 – Final Instructions," Enduring Word, https://enduringword.com/bible-commentary/galatians-6/.

Week 6: Day 4

1. Darrell L. Bock, *Ephesians: An Introduction and Commentary*, ed. Eckhard J. Schnabel and Nicholas Perrin, vol. 10, Tyndale New Testament Commentaries (InterVarsity Press, 2019), 44.

Week 7: Day 5

1. "Ephesians 3 – The Revealing of God's Mystery," Enduring Word, https://enduringword.com/bible-commentary/ephesians-3/.

Week 8: Day 2

1. John Stott, *The Message of Ephesians* (InterVarsity Press, 1979), 172.

Week 8: Day 3

1. Kenneth L. Barker and John R. Kohlenberger, III, ed., *Zondervan NIV Bible Commentary*, vol. 2 (Zondervan, 1999), 771.

Week 8: Day 4

1. John Stott, *The Message of Ephesians* (InterVarsity Press, 1979), 185.
2. John Stott, *The Message of Ephesians* (InterVarsity Press, 1979), 185.

Week 9: Day 1

1. Tremper Longman III and David E. Garland, ed., *The Expositor's Bible Commentary: Ephesians–Philemon*, rev. ed., vol. 12 (Zondervan Academic, 2006), 133.

Week 9: Day 2

1. *ESV Women's Study Bible* (Crossway, 2020), 1946n5:14.
2. "Ephesians 5 – Life in the Spirit," Enduring Word, https://enduringword.com/bible-commentary/ephesians-5/.
3. *The Expositor's Bible Commentary: Ephesians–Philemon, Revised edition* (Zondervan Academic, 2006), 138.
4. *The Expositor's Bible Commentary: Ephesians–Philemon, Revised edition* (Zondervan Academic, 2006), 138.

Week 9: Day 4

1. *The Expositor's Bible Commentary: Ephesians–Philemon, Revised edition* (Zondervan Academic, 2006), 147.

Week 9: Day 5

1. *The Expositor's Bible Commentary: Ephesians–Philemon, Revised edition* (Zondervan Academic, 2006), 151.

ABOUT THE EDITOR

TARA-LEIGH COBBLE'S zeal for biblical literacy is at the heart of everything she creates. Her goal is to help people read, understand, and love the Bible. Her daily podcast, *The Bible Recap*, guides listeners through a chronological one-year reading plan. The podcast has over 500 million downloads and reached number one on the Apple Podcast charts in All Categories. She created and leads D-Group International, which has grown into an international network of nearly 400 weekly Bible studies that meet in homes, in churches, and online. A *Wall Street Journal* bestselling author, she also writes and hosts a daily radio feature called *The God Shot*, and leads trips to Israel to study the Bible on-site. Tara-Leigh lives in Dallas, Texas, where she has no pets, children, or anything else that might die if she forgets to feed it.

For more information: TaraLeighCobble.com | TheBibleRecap.com | MyDGroup.org | Israelux.com
Social media: @taraleighcobble | @thebiblerecap | @mydgroup | @israeluxtours

MINISTRIES

THE BIBLE RECAP—*READ THE BIBLE*

Est. 2019 | TheBibleRecap.com
Have you ever closed your Bible and thought, *What did I just read?* In about eight minutes a day, our summary walks you through the one-year chronological plan. Available in podcast, YouTube, and book form. Other supplemental resources available for adults and children.

D-GROUP INTERNATIONAL—*STUDY THE BIBLE*

Est. 2009 | MyDGroup.org
Men's and women's Bible study groups that meet weekly—in homes, online, and in churches around the world. D-Groups work through a series of 40 studies that cover the entire Bible over the course of a decade.

ISRAELUX—*EXPERIENCE THE BIBLE*

Est. 2014 | Israelux.com
Offering a deluxe tour, incredible dining experiences, luxury accommodations, and life-changing teaching at biblical sites. The beauty of Israel is also captured in TLC's book *Israel: Beauty, Light, and Luxury*, a *Wall Street Journal* bestseller.